Math Expressions

Volume 2

Developed by
The Children's Math Worlds Research Project

PROJECT DIRECTOR AND AUTHOR
Dr. Karen C. Fuson

This material is based upon work supported by the
National Science Foundation
under Grant Numbers
ESI-9816320, REC-9806020, and RED-935373.

Any opinions, findings, and conclusions, or recommendations expressed in this material
are those of the author and do not necessarily reflect the views of the National Science Foundation.

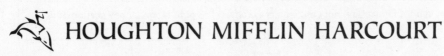

HOUGHTON MIFFLIN HARCOURT

Teacher Reviewers

Kindergarten

Patricia Stroh Sugiyama
Wilmette, Illinois

Barbara Wahle
Evanston, Illinois

Grade 1

Sandra Budson
Newton, Massachusetts

Janet Pecci
Chicago, Illinois

Megan Rees
Chicago, Illinois

Grade 2

Molly Dunn
Danvers, Massachusetts

Agnes Lesnick
Hillside, Illinois

Rita Soto
Chicago, Illinois

Grade 3

Jane Curran
Honesdale, Pennsylvania

Sandra Tucker
Chicago, Illinois

Grade 4

Sara Stoneberg Llibre
Chicago, Illinois

Sheri Roedel
Chicago, Illinois

Grade 5

Todd Atler
Chicago, Illinois

Leah Barry
Norfolk, Massachusetts

Special Thanks

Special thanks to the many teachers, students, parents, principals, writers, researchers, and work-study students who participated in the Children's Math Worlds Research Project over the years.

Credits

Cover art: © Kerstin Layer/Age Fotostock

Illustrative art: Robin Boyer/Deborah Wolfe, LTD; Dave Clegg, Geoff Smith, Ron Mahoney, Tim Johnson
Technical art: Nesbitt Graphics, Inc.
Photos: Nesbitt Graphics, Inc.; Page 93 © C Squared Studios/Photodisc/Getty Images; Page 455 © Nick Green/Jupiter Images

2011 Edition
Copyright © 2009 by Houghton Mifflin Harcourt Publishing Company

Printed in the U.S.A.

ISBN: 978-0-547-47379-6

1 2 3 4 5 6 7 8 9 10   1421   19 18 17 16 15 14 13 12 11 10

4500228424   X B C D E

VOLUME 2 CONTENTS

Name _____ **Date** _____

Class Activity

▶ Solve Area and Perimeter Problems

Read the problem below and complete exercises 12 and 13.

> Debra wants to tile the floor of a rectangular room in her house. The floor is 9 feet long and 8 feet wide. The tiles are squares with sides that are 1 foot long. How many tiles does she need?
>
>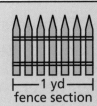

12. To find the total number of tiles, do you need to find the perimeter or area of the room? Explain.

_____

_____

_____

13. How many tiles does Debra need? _____

Read the problem below and complete exercises 14 and 15.

> Deshawn wants to build a fence around a rectangular space in his backyard. The space is 5 yards long and 3 yards wide. The fence sections are 1 yard long. How many fence sections does Deshawn need?
>
> ├—1 yd—┤
> fence section

14. To find the number of fence sections, do you need to find the perimeter or area of the rectangle? Explain.

_____

_____

_____

15. How many fence sections does Deshawn need? _____

16. **Math Journal** Create and solve a word problem that involves finding the area of a figure. Draw a picture to show your answer is correct.

Class Activity

▶ Estimate Perimeter and Area

17. Estimate the perimeter of an index card and CD case in centimeters. Record your estimates in the table. Then find the actual perimeters.

18. Estimate the area of an index card and CD case in centimeters. Record your estimates in the table. Then find the actual areas using a calculator.

Object	Perimeter		Area	
	Estimate (cm)	Actual (cm)	Estimate (cm²)	Actual (cm²)
Index card				
CD case				

▶ Estimate the Perimeter and Area of Irregular Figures

19. Use centimeter grid paper (TRB M31). Trace your hand with fingers together and thumb out on the grid. Estimate the perimeter and area.

Perimeter: About _____ cm   Area: About _____ cm²

Class Activity

▶ Explore Patterns with 6s

What patterns do you see below?

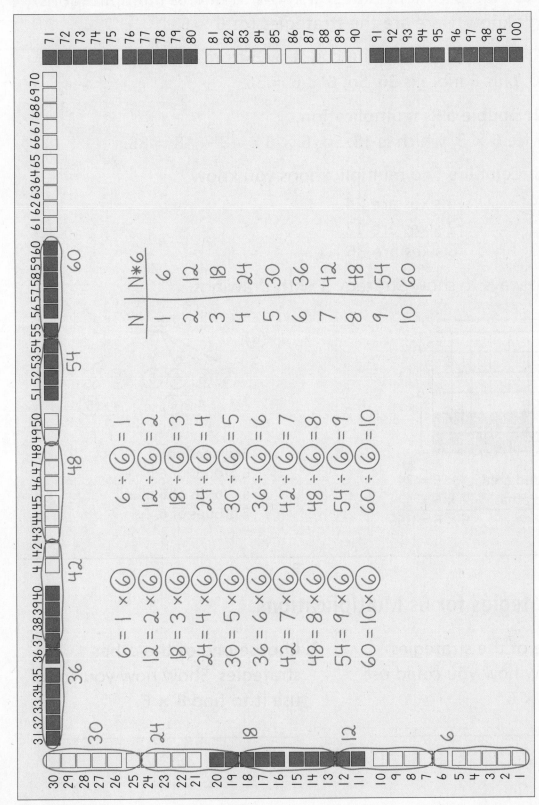

▶ Strategies for Multiplying with 6

You can use 6s multiplications that you know to find 6s multiplications that you don't know. Here are the strategies for 6 × 6.

- **Strategy 1:** Start with 5 × 6, and count by 6 from there.
  5 × 6 = 30, plus 6 more is 36. So, 6 × 6 = 36.

- **Strategy 2:** Double a 3s multiplication.
  6 × 6 is twice 6 × 3, which is 18. So, 6 × 6 = 18 + 18 = 36.

- **Strategy 3:** Combine two multiplications you know.

4 × 6 = 24	4 sixes are 24.
2 × 6 = 12	2 sixes are 12.
6 × 6 = 36	6 sixes are 36.

Here are two ways to show Strategy 3 with drawings.

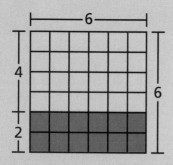

unshaded area: 4 × 6 = 24
shaded area: 2 × 6 = 12
total area: 6 × 6 = 36

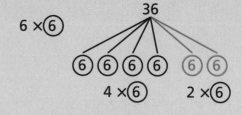

Explanation:
6 groups of 6 is
4 groups of 6 plus
2 groups of 6.

▶ Apply Strategies for 6s Multiplications

1. Choose one of the strategies above. Show how you could use it to find 7 × 6.

2. Choose one of the other strategies. Show how you could use it to find 8 × 6.

Dear Family,

In this unit, students learn multiplications and divisions for 6s, 7s, and 8s, while continuing to practice the rest of the basic multiplications and divisions covered in Unit 4.

Although students practice all the 6s, 7s, and 8s multiplications, they really have only six new multiplications to learn: 6×6, 6×7, 6×8, 7×7, 7×8, and 8×8. The lessons for these multiplications focus on strategies for finding the products using multiplications they know.

Students are also introduced to comparisons involving multiplication and division. Such comparisons involve one quantity that is a number of times *as many as* or *as much as* another. Here are two examples:

- Teresa has 2 gerbils. Owen has 4 times as many gerbils as Teresa has. How many gerbils does Owen have?

- Eduardo has 12 posters in his room. Manuela has $\frac{1}{3}$ as many posters as Eduardo. How many posters does Manuela have?

This unit also focuses on word problems. Students are presented with a variety of one-step word problems. They use the language and context of each problem to determine which operation—multiplication, division, addition, or subtraction—they must use to solve it. Students solve multi-step problems using a variety of methods.

Please continue to help your child get faster on multiplications and divisions. Use all of the practice materials that your child has brought home. Your support is crucial to your child's learning.

Please call if you have any questions or comments.

Thank you.

Sincerely,
Your child's teacher

Estimada familia:

En esta unidad los estudiantes aprenden las multiplicaciones y divisiones con el 6, el 7 y el 8, mientras siguen practicando las demás multiplicaciones y divisiones que se presentaron en la Unidad 4.

Aunque los estudiantes practican todas las multiplicaciones con el 6, el 7 y el 8, en realidad sólo tienen que aprender seis multiplicaciones nuevas: 6×6, 6×7, 6×8, 7×7, 7×8 y 8×8. Las lecciones de estas multiplicaciones se centran en estrategias para hallar los productos usando multiplicaciones que ya se conocen.

Los estudiantes también empiezan a hacer comparaciones de cantidades que resultan de la multiplicación y la división. Las comparaciones de este tipo tratan de una cantidad que es *tantas veces*. Aquí hay dos ejemplos:

- Teresa tiene 2 gerbos. Owen tiene 4 veces más gerbos que Teresa. ¿Cuántos gerbos tiene Owen?

- Eduardo tiene 12 carteles en su cuarto. Manuela tiene $\frac{1}{3}$ del número de carteles que tiene Eduardo. ¿Cuántos carteles tiene Manuela?

Esta unidad también se centra en problemas verbales. A los estudiantes se les presenta una varidad de problemas verbales de un paso. Aprovechan el lenguaje y el contexto de cada problema para determinar qué operación deben usar para resolverlo: la multiplicación, la división, la suma o la resta. Los estudiantes también resuelven problemas de varios pasos utilizando una variedad de métodos.

Por favor continúe ayudando a su niño a practicar las multiplicaciones y las divisiones. Use todos los materiales de práctica que su niño ha llevado a casa. Su apoyo es importante para el aprendizaje de su niño.

Si tiene alguna duda o pregunta, por favor comuníquese conmigo.

Atentamente,
El maestro de su niño

Multiply and Divide with 6

Study Sheet C

7s

Count-bys	Mixed Up ×	Mixed Up ÷
1 × 7 = 7	6 × 7 = 42	70 ÷ 7 = 10
2 × 7 = 14	8 × 7 = 56	14 ÷ 7 = 2
3 × 7 = 21	5 × 7 = 35	28 ÷ 7 = 4
4 × 7 = 28	9 × 7 = 63	56 ÷ 7 = 8
5 × 7 = 35	4 × 7 = 28	42 ÷ 7 = 6
6 × 7 = 42	10 × 7 = 70	63 ÷ 7 = 9
7 × 7 = 49	3 × 7 = 21	21 ÷ 7 = 3
8 × 7 = 56	1 × 7 = 7	49 ÷ 7 = 7
9 × 7 = 63	7 × 7 = 49	7 ÷ 7 = 1
10 × 7 = 70	2 × 7 = 14	35 ÷ 7 = 5

6s

Count-bys	Mixed Up ×	Mixed Up ÷
1 × 6 = 6	10 × 6 = 60	54 ÷ 6 = 9
2 × 6 = 12	8 × 6 = 48	30 ÷ 6 = 5
3 × 6 = 18	2 × 6 = 12	12 ÷ 6 = 2
4 × 6 = 24	6 × 6 = 36	60 ÷ 6 = 10
5 × 6 = 30	4 × 6 = 24	48 ÷ 6 = 8
6 × 6 = 36	1 × 6 = 6	36 ÷ 6 = 6
7 × 6 = 42	9 × 6 = 54	6 ÷ 6 = 1
8 × 6 = 48	3 × 6 = 18	42 ÷ 6 = 7
9 × 6 = 54	7 × 6 = 42	18 ÷ 6 = 3
10 × 6 = 60	5 × 6 = 30	24 ÷ 6 = 4

Squares

Count-bys	Mixed Up ×	Mixed Up ÷
1 × 1 = 1	3 × 3 = 9	25 ÷ 5 = 5
2 × 2 = 4	9 × 9 = 81	4 ÷ 2 = 2
3 × 3 = 9	4 × 4 = 16	81 ÷ 9 = 9
4 × 4 = 16	6 × 6 = 36	9 ÷ 3 = 3
5 × 5 = 25	2 × 2 = 4	36 ÷ 6 = 6
6 × 6 = 36	7 × 7 = 49	100 ÷ 10 = 10
7 × 7 = 49	10 × 10 = 100	16 ÷ 4 = 4
8 × 8 = 64	1 × 1 = 1	49 ÷ 7 = 7
9 × 9 = 81	5 × 5 = 25	1 ÷ 1 = 1
10 × 10 = 100	8 × 8 = 64	64 ÷ 8 = 8

8s

Count-bys	Mixed Up ×	Mixed Up ÷
1 × 8 = 8	6 × 8 = 48	16 ÷ 8 = 2
2 × 8 = 16	10 × 8 = 80	40 ÷ 8 = 5
3 × 8 = 24	7 × 8 = 56	72 ÷ 8 = 9
4 × 8 = 32	2 × 8 = 16	32 ÷ 8 = 4
5 × 8 = 40	4 × 8 = 32	8 ÷ 8 = 1
6 × 8 = 48	8 × 8 = 64	80 ÷ 8 = 10
7 × 8 = 56	5 × 8 = 40	64 ÷ 8 = 8
8 × 8 = 64	10 × 8 = 80	24 ÷ 8 = 3
9 × 8 = 72	3 × 8 = 24	56 ÷ 8 = 7
10 × 8 = 80	1 × 8 = 8	48 ÷ 8 = 6

Study Sheet C

Name _____ Date _____

► Missing Number Puzzles

Complete each Missing Number puzzle.

1.

×	5	2	
	30		48
4		8	32
	45		72

2.

×		3	
6	30		42
4			28
	40	24	56

3.

×	4		8
9		81	
	12		24
	20	45	40

► Solve and Discuss Area Word Problems

Solve each problem. Label your answers with the correct units.

Show your work.

4. The mattress has a length of 7 feet and a width of 6 feet. What is the area of the mattress?

_____

5. The wading pool at Evans Park is shaped like a square with sides 8 feet long. What is the area of the wading pool?

_____

6. Milo's rug has a length of 5 feet and an area of 40 square feet. What is the width of his rug?

_____

7. Lana wants to enclose a garden plot with a piece of rope that is 36 feet long. Lana wants to have the most space possible for gardening. Draw a picture of what Lana's garden will look like. Label the drawing.

Going Further

▶Problem-Solving Strategy: Draw a Picture

Draw a picture to help solve each problem.

1. Ana has a ribbon that is 18 inches long. She cut the ribbon into 3 equal pieces. Then she cut each of those pieces in half. How many small pieces of ribbon are there? How long is each piece?

   _____

2. A sign is shaped like a square. Eva draws lines in the sign to make 3 equal rectangles. Each rectangle is 3 inches wide and 9 inches long. What is the area of the square?

   _____

3. Ty puts up a 20-foot-long fence to make a rectangular garden. He divides the rectangle into 4 equal squares all in one row. The side of each square is 2 feet long. What is the area of the garden?

   _____

4. Aaron is stacking cans in a grocery store. The bottom row has 7 cans. Each row above has 1 fewer can. How many cans will be stacked in all?

   _____

5. There are 4 cars in a row. Each car is 13 feet long. There are 6 feet between each car. What is the length from the front of the first car to the back of the last car in the row?

   _____

Solve Area Word Problems

▶Check Sheet 8: 6s and 8s

6s Multiplications	6s Divisions	8s Multiplications	8s Divisions
$10 \times 6 = 60$	$24 / 6 = 4$	$2 \times 8 = 16$	$72 / 8 = 9$
$6 \cdot 4 = 24$	$48 \div 6 = 8$	$8 \cdot 10 = 80$	$16 \div 8 = 2$
$6 * 7 = 42$	$60 / 6 = 10$	$3 * 8 = 24$	$40 / 8 = 5$
$2 \times 6 = 12$	$12 \div 6 = 2$	$9 \times 8 = 72$	$8 \div 8 = 1$
$6 \cdot 5 = 30$	$42 / 6 = 7$	$8 \cdot 4 = 32$	$80 / 8 = 10$
$6 * 8 = 48$	$30 \div 6 = 5$	$8 * 7 = 56$	$48 \div 8 = 6$
$9 \times 6 = 54$	$6 / 6 = 1$	$5 \times 8 = 40$	$56 / 8 = 7$
$6 \cdot 1 = 6$	$18 \div 6 = 3$	$8 \cdot 6 = 48$	$24 \div 8 = 3$
$6 * 6 = 36$	$54 / 6 = 9$	$1 * 8 = 8$	$64 / 8 = 8$
$6 \times 3 = 18$	$36 / 6 = 6$	$8 \times 8 = 64$	$32 / 8 = 4$
$6 \cdot 6 = 36$	$48 \div 6 = 8$	$4 \cdot 8 = 32$	$80 \div 8 = 10$
$5 * 6 = 30$	$12 / 6 = 2$	$6 * 8 = 48$	$56 / 8 = 7$
$6 \times 2 = 12$	$24 \div 6 = 4$	$8 \times 3 = 24$	$8 \div 8 = 1$
$4 \cdot 6 = 24$	$60 / 6 = 10$	$7 \cdot 8 = 56$	$24 / 8 = 3$
$6 * 9 = 54$	$6 \div 6 = 1$	$8 * 2 = 16$	$64 \div 8 = 8$
$8 \times 6 = 48$	$42 / 6 = 7$	$8 \times 9 = 72$	$16 / 8 = 2$
$7 \cdot 6 = 42$	$18 \div 6 = 3$	$8 \cdot 1 = 8$	$72 \div 8 = 9$
$6 * 10 = 60$	$36 \div 6 = 6$	$8 * 8 = 64$	$32 \div 8 = 4$
$1 \times 6 = 6$	$30 / 6 = 5$	$10 \times 8 = 80$	$40 / 8 = 5$
$4 \cdot 6 = 24$	$54 \div 6 = 9$	$5 \cdot 8 = 40$	$48 \div 8 = 6$

Check Sheet 8: 6s and 8s

Class Activity

▶ **Explore Patterns with 8s.**

What patterns do you see below?

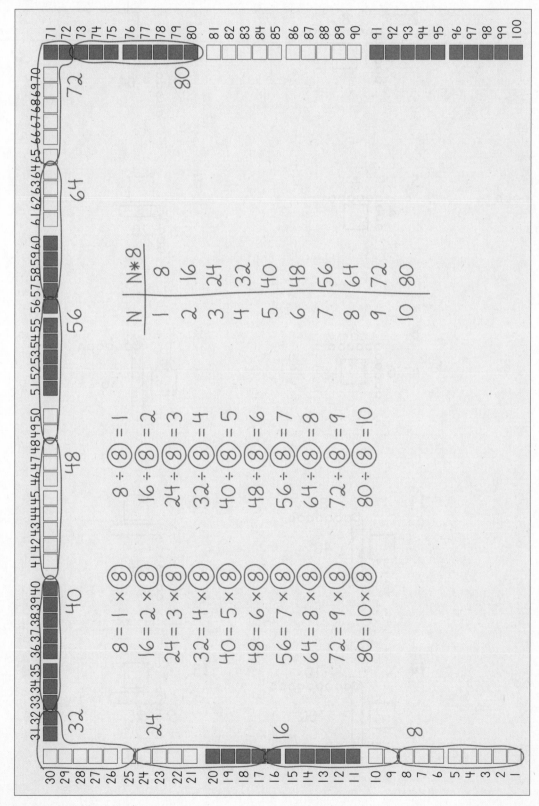

Multiply and Divide with 8 **311**

Name

Date

Class Activity

▶ Fast-Array Drawings

Find the missing number for each Fast-Array drawing.

1.   6
⬜ 42

2.   8
6 ⬜

3.   ⬜
8 64

4.   9
⬜ 63

5.   6
4 ⬜

6.   ⬜
5 20

7.   ⬜
9 45

8.   6
6 ⬜

9.   7
⬜ 56

10.   7
7 ⬜

11.   8
⬜ 40

12.   ⬜
8 24

13.   9
8 ⬜

14.   10
⬜ 100

15.   ⬜
5 25

Multiply and Divide with 8

▶ **Sprints for 6s**

As your teacher reads each multiplication or division, write your answer in the space provided.

× 6	÷ 6
a. _____	a. _____
b. _____	b. _____
c. _____	c. _____
d. _____	d. _____
e. _____	e. _____
f. _____	f. _____
g. _____	g. _____
h. _____	h. _____
i. _____	i. _____
j. _____	j. _____

▶Identify the Type and Choose the Operation

Solve. Then circle what type it is and what operation you use.

1. Students in Mr. Till's class hung their paintings on the wall. They made 6 rows, with 5 paintings in each row. How many paintings did the students hang?

   _____

   Circle one: array   repeated groups   area
   Circle one: multiplication   division

2. Write your own problem that is the same type as problem 1. _____

   _____

   _____

3. There are 8 goldfish in each tank at the pet store. If there are 56 goldfish in all, how many tanks are there?

   _____

   Circle one: array   repeated groups   area
   Circle one: multiplication   division

4. Write your own problem that is the same type as problem 3. _____

   _____

   _____

5. Pierre built a rectangular pen for his rabbits. The pen is 4 feet wide and 6 feet long. What is the area of the pen? _____

   Circle one: array   repeated groups   area
   Circle one: multiplication   division

Write Word Problems and Equations

6. Write your own problem that is the same type as problem 5. _____

_____

_____

Solve the word problem. Then circle what type it is and circle the operation you would use.

7. Paulo arranged 72 baseball cards in 9 rows and a certain number of columns. How many columns did he arrange the cards into? _____

   Circle one: array   repeated groups   area
   Circle one: multiplication   division

8. Write your own problem that is the same type as Problem 7. _____

_____

_____

9. The store sells bottles of juice in six-packs. Mr. Lee bought 9 six-packs for a picnic. How many bottles did he buy? _____

   Circle one: array   repeated groups   area
   Circle one: multiplication   division

10. Write your own problem that is the same type as Problem 9. _____

_____

_____

11. **Math Journal** Write an area multiplication problem. Draw a Fast Array to solve it.

Name _____ **Date** _____

Class Activity

Vocabulary

equation
variable

▶ Use Variables in Equations

When you write **equations** you can use a letter to represent an unknown number. This letter is called a **variable**.

These equations have variables.

$a + 4 = 6$	$7 = c + 3$	$w = 8 - 3$	$9 = 18 - c$
$6 \times y = 18$	$p = 6 \times 3$	$f = 18 \div 3$	$18 \div n = 3$

Solve each equation.

13. $21 = 7 \times a$

   $a =$ _____

14. $63 \div g = 9$

   $g =$ _____

15. $10 - n = 6$

   $n =$ _____

16. $8 + f = 13$

   $f =$ _____

▶ Write and Solve Equations with Variables

Write an equation for each word problem. Then solve the equation.

17. A large box of crayons holds 60 crayons. There are 10 crayons in each row. How many rows are there?

_____

18. A poster covers 12 square feet. The poster is 4 feet long. How wide is the poster?

_____

19. There are 7 groups of students with an equal number of students in each group working on a social studies project. There are 28 students working on the project. How many students are there in each group?

_____

20. Amanda has 15 bracelets. She gave a number of bracelets to friends. She has 10 bracelets left. How many bracelets did she give to friends?

_____

Write Word Problems and Equations

Class Activity

Name

Date

▶ Explore Patterns with 7s

What patterns do you see below?

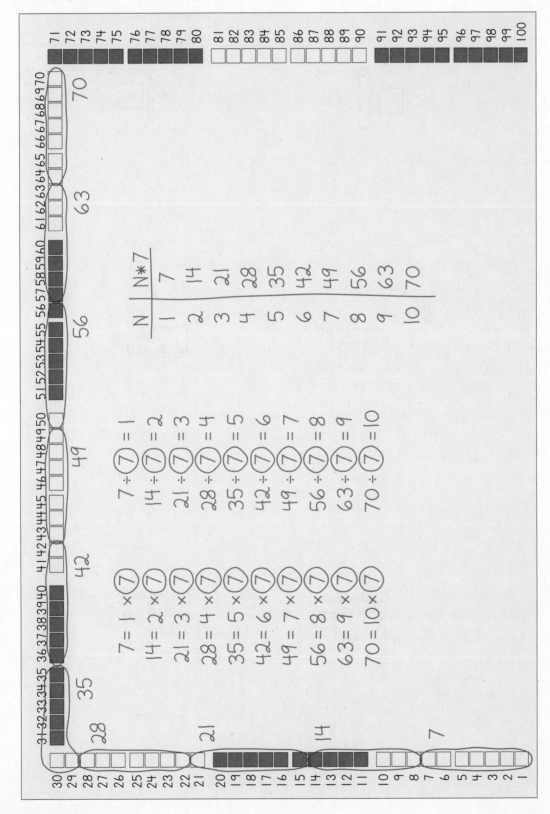

N	N*7
1	7
2	14
3	21
4	28
5	35
6	42
7	49
8	56
9	63
10	70

$7 ÷ ⑦ = 1$

$14 ÷ ⑦ = 2$

$21 ÷ ⑦ = 3$

$28 ÷ ⑦ = 4$

$35 ÷ ⑦ = 5$

$42 ÷ ⑦ = 6$

$49 ÷ ⑦ = 7$

$56 ÷ ⑦ = 8$

$63 ÷ ⑦ = 9$

$70 ÷ ⑦ = 10$

$7 = 1 × ⑦$

$14 = 2 × ⑦$

$21 = 3 × ⑦$

$28 = 4 × ⑦$

$35 = 5 × ⑦$

$42 = 6 × ⑦$

$49 = 7 × ⑦$

$56 = 8 × ⑦$

$63 = 9 × ⑦$

$70 = 10 × ⑦$

Class Activity

► More Fast-Array Drawings

Fill in the missing number in each Fast-Array Drawing.

1.

7

4 ☐

2.

7

☐ 42

3.

5

6 ☐

4.

☐

3 24

5.

8

6 ☐

6.

☐ 5

10

7.

6

☐ 36

8.

☐

8 56

9.

4

3 ☐

Multiply and Divide with 7

▶Dashes 5–8

Complete each multiplication and division Dash.
Check your answers on page 321.

Dash 5 2s, 5s, 9s, 10s Multiplications	Dash 6 2s, 5s, 9s, 10s Divisions	Dash 7 0s, 1s, 3s, 4s Multiplications	Dash 8 1s, 3s, 4s Divisions
a. $6 \times 2 =$ ___	a. $18 / 2 =$ ___	a. $7 \times 1 =$ ___	a. $2 / 1 =$ ___
b. $9 \cdot 4 =$ ___	b. $25 \div 5 =$ ___	b. $0 \cdot 6 =$ ___	b. $28 \div 4 =$ ___
c. $8 * 5 =$ ___	c. $70 / 10 =$ ___	c. $4 * 4 =$ ___	c. $3 / 3 =$ ___
d. $1 \times 10 =$ ___	d. $54 \div 9 =$ ___	d. $7 \times 3 =$ ___	d. $1 \div 1 =$ ___
e. $2 \cdot 7 =$ ___	e. $50 / 5 =$ ___	e. $3 \cdot 1 =$ ___	e. $40 / 4 =$ ___
f. $9 * 9 =$ ___	f. $81 \div 9 =$ ___	f. $4 * 7 =$ ___	f. $21 \div 3 =$ ___
g. $5 \times 6 =$ ___	g. $8 / 2 =$ ___	g. $9 \times 0 =$ ___	g. $5 / 1 =$ ___
h. $10 \cdot 4 =$ ___	h. $90 \div 10 =$ ___	h. $1 \cdot 1 =$ ___	h. $16 \div 4 =$ ___
i. $7 * 5 =$ ___	i. $35 / 5 =$ ___	i. $3 * 4 =$ ___	i. $15 / 3 =$ ___
j. $8 \times 2 =$ ___	j. $27 / 9 =$ ___	j. $4 \times 9 =$ ___	j. $6 / 1 =$ ___
k. $10 \cdot 10 =$ ___	k. $2 \div 2 =$ ___	k. $8 \cdot 1 =$ ___	k. $12 \div 4 =$ ___
l. $5 * 3 =$ ___	l. $36 / 9 =$ ___	l. $3 * 3 =$ ___	l. $27 / 3 =$ ___
m. $9 \times 7 =$ ___	m. $45 \div 5 =$ ___	m. $0 \times 4 =$ ___	m. $9 \div 1 =$ ___
n. $9 \cdot 2 =$ ___	n. $14 / 2 =$ ___	n. $10 \cdot 3 =$ ___	n. $8 / 4 =$ ___
o. $5 * 5 =$ ___	o. $20 \div 10 =$ ___	o. $6 * 4 =$ ___	o. $12 \div 3 =$ ___
p. $6 \times 9 =$ ___	p. $9 / 9 =$ ___	p. $1 \times 4 =$ ___	p. $3 / 1 =$ ___
q. $5 \cdot 2 =$ ___	q. $20 \div 5 =$ ___	q. $3 \cdot 6 =$ ___	q. $36 \div 4 =$ ___
r. $9 * 5 =$ ___	r. $45 \div 9 =$ ___	r. $4 * 8 =$ ___	r. $6 \div 3 =$ ___
s. $8 \times 10 =$ ___	s. $5 / 5 =$ ___	s. $7 \times 0 =$ ___	s. $4 / 1 =$ ___
t. $5 \cdot 10 =$ ___	t. $4 \div 2 =$ ___	t. $5 \cdot 3 =$ ___	t. $4 \div 4 =$ ___

▶ Dashes 5–8

**Complete each multiplication and division Dash.
Check your answers on page 321.**

Dash 5 **2s, 5s, 9s, 10s** **Multiplications**	**Dash 6** **2s, 5s, 9s, 10s** **Divisions**	**Dash 7** **0s, 1s, 3s, 4s** **Multiplications**	**Dash 8** **1s, 3s, 4s** **Divisions**
a. $6 \times 2 =$ ___	a. $18 / 2 =$ ___	a. $7 \times 1 =$ ___	a. $2 / 1 =$ ___
b. $9 \cdot 4 =$ ___	b. $25 \div 5 =$ ___	b. $0 \cdot 6 =$ ___	b. $28 \div 4 =$ ___
c. $8 * 5 =$ ___	c. $70 / 10 =$ ___	c. $4 * 4 =$ ___	c. $3 / 3 =$ ___
d. $1 \times 10 =$ ___	d. $54 \div 9 =$ ___	d. $7 \times 3 =$ ___	d. $1 \div 1 =$ ___
e. $2 \cdot 7 =$ ___	e. $50 / 5 =$ ___	e. $3 \cdot 1 =$ ___	e. $40 / 4 =$ ___
f. $9 * 9 =$ ___	f. $81 \div 9 =$ ___	f. $4 * 7 =$ ___	f. $21 \div 3 =$ ___
g. $5 \times 6 =$ ___	g. $8 / 2 =$ ___	g. $9 \times 0 =$ ___	g. $5 / 1 =$ ___
h. $10 \cdot 4 =$ ___	h. $90 \div 10 =$ ___	h. $1 \cdot 1 =$ ___	h. $16 \div 4 =$ ___
i. $7 * 5 =$ ___	i. $35 / 5 =$ ___	i. $3 * 4 =$ ___	i. $15 / 3 =$ ___
j. $8 \times 2 =$ ___	j. $27 / 9 =$ ___	j. $4 \times 9 =$ ___	j. $6 / 1 =$ ___
k. $10 \cdot 10 =$ ___	k. $2 \div 2 =$ ___	k. $8 \cdot 1 =$ ___	k. $12 \div 4 =$ ___
l. $5 * 3 =$ ___	l. $36 / 9 =$ ___	l. $3 * 3 =$ ___	l. $27 / 3 =$ ___
m. $9 \times 7 =$ ___	m. $45 \div 5 =$ ___	m. $0 \times 4 =$ ___	m. $9 \div 1 =$ ___
n. $9 \cdot 2 =$ ___	n. $14 / 2 =$ ___	n. $10 \cdot 3 =$ ___	n. $8 / 4 =$ ___
o. $5 * 5 =$ ___	o. $20 \div 10 =$ ___	o. $6 * 4 =$ ___	o. $12 \div 3 =$ ___
p. $6 \times 9 =$ ___	p. $9 / 9 =$ ___	p. $1 \times 4 =$ ___	p. $3 / 1 =$ ___
q. $5 \cdot 2 =$ ___	q. $20 \div 5 =$ ___	q. $3 \cdot 6 =$ ___	q. $36 \div 4 =$ ___
r. $9 * 5 =$ ___	r. $45 \div 9 =$ ___	r. $4 * 8 =$ ___	r. $6 \div 3 =$ ___
s. $8 \times 10 =$ ___	s. $5 / 5 =$ ___	s. $7 \times 0 =$ ___	s. $4 / 1 =$ ___
t. $5 \cdot 10 =$ ___	t. $4 \div 2 =$ ___	t. $5 \cdot 3 =$ ___	t. $4 \div 4 =$ ___

▶Answers to Dashes 5–8

Use this sheet to check your answers to the Dashes on page 319.

Dash 5 2s, 5s, 9s, 10s Multiplications	Dash 6 2s, 5s, 9s, 10s Divisions	Dash 7 0s, 1s, 3s, 4s Multiplications	Dash 8 1s, 3s, 4s Divisions
a. $6 \times 2 = 12$	a. $18 / 2 = 9$	a. $7 \times 1 = 7$	a. $2 / 1 = 2$
b. $9 \cdot 4 = 36$	b. $25 \div 5 = 5$	b. $0 \cdot 6 = 0$	b. $28 \div 4 = 7$
c. $8 * 5 = 40$	c. $70 / 10 = 7$	c. $4 * 4 = 16$	c. $3 / 3 = 1$
d. $1 \times 10 = 10$	d. $54 \div 9 = 6$	d. $7 \times 3 = 21$	d. $1 \div 1 = 1$
e. $2 \cdot 7 = 14$	e. $50 / 5 = 10$	e. $3 \cdot 1 = 3$	e. $40 / 4 = 10$
f. $9 * 9 = 81$	f. $81 \div 9 = 9$	f. $4 * 7 = 28$	f. $21 \div 3 = 7$
g. $5 \times 6 = 30$	g. $8 / 2 = 4$	g. $9 \times 0 = 0$	g. $5 / 1 = 5$
h. $10 \cdot 4 = 40$	h. $90 \div 10 = 9$	h. $1 \cdot 1 = 1$	h. $16 \div 4 = 4$
i. $7 * 5 = 35$	i. $35 / 5 = 7$	i. $3 * 4 = 12$	i. $15 / 3 = 5$
j. $8 \times 2 = 16$	j. $27 / 9 = 3$	j. $4 \times 9 = 36$	j. $6 / 1 = 6$
k. $10 \cdot 10 = 100$	k. $2 \div 2 = 1$	k. $8 \cdot 1 = 8$	k. $12 \div 4 = 3$
l. $5 * 3 = 15$	l. $36 / 9 = 4$	l. $3 * 3 = 9$	l. $27 / 3 = 9$
m. $9 \times 7 = 63$	m. $45 \div 5 = 9$	m. $0 \times 4 = 0$	m. $9 \div 1 = 9$
n. $9 \cdot 2 = 18$	n. $14 / 2 = 7$	n. $10 \cdot 3 = 30$	n. $8 / 4 = 2$
o. $5 * 5 = 25$	o. $20 \div 10 = 2$	o. $6 * 4 = 24$	o. $12 \div 3 = 4$
p. $6 \times 9 = 54$	p. $9 / 9 = 1$	p. $1 \times 4 = 4$	p. $3 / 1 = 3$
q. $5 \cdot 2 = 10$	q. $20 \div 5 = 4$	q. $3 \cdot 6 = 18$	q. $36 \div 4 = 9$
r. $9 * 5 = 45$	r. $45 \div 9 = 5$	r. $4 * 8 = 32$	r. $6 \div 3 = 2$
s. $8 \times 10 = 80$	s. $5 / 5 = 1$	s. $7 \times 0 = 0$	s. $4 / 1 = 4$
t. $5 \cdot 10 = 50$	t. $4 \div 2 = 2$	t. $5 \cdot 3 = 15$	t. $4 \div 4 = 1$

Answers to Dashes 5–8

▶ Comparison Statements

Use the sentences and pictures below to complete the comparison statements.

> Martina has 6 tennis balls. Chris has 2 tennis balls.

Martina

Chris

1. Martina has _____ more tennis balls than Chris.

2. Chris has _____ fewer tennis balls than Martina.

3. Martina has _____ times as many tennis balls as Chris.

4. Chris has _____ as many tennis balls as Martina.

Use the sentences and pictures below to complete the comparison statements.

> Bobby has 3 hockey pucks. Wayne has 15 hockey pucks.

Bobby

Wayne

5. Write a comparison statement about the hockey pucks using the word *more.*

_____

6. Write a comparison statement about the hockey pucks using the word *fewer.*

_____

7. Wayne has _____ times as many hockey pucks as Bobby.

8. Bobby has _____ as many hockey pucks as Wayne.

Make a math drawing to show the situation. Then use the sentences to write and complete the comparison statements.

Abby has 8 comic books. Pascal has 2 comic books.

9. Write a comparison statement about the comic books using the word *more.*

_____

10. Write a comparison statement about the comic books using the word *fewer.*

_____

11. Abby has _____ as many comic books as Pascal.

12. Pascal has _____ as many comic books as Abby.

Kai has 3 paintbrushes. Neeta has 18 paintbrushes.

13. Write a comparison statement about the paintbrushes using the word *more.*

_____

14. Write a comparison statement about the paintbrushes using the word *fewer.*

_____

15. Kai has _____ as many paint brushes as Neeta.

16. Neeta has _____ as many paint brushes as Kai.

Comparison Word Problems

►Solve Comparison Word Problems

Solve each problem.

17. Teresa has 2 gerbils. Owen has 4 times as many gerbils as Teresa has. How many gerbils does Owen have? _____

18. Eduardo has 12 posters in his room. Manuela has $\frac{1}{3}$ as many posters as Eduardo. How many posters does Manuela have? _____

19. Bart rides his bike 8 blocks to school. Melinda rides 5 times as far as Bart does. How many blocks does Melinda ride? _____

20. Jay ate 14 grapes. Ti ate $\frac{1}{7}$ as many grapes as Jay. How many grapes did Ti eat? _____

21. Lucille has 7 books. Javier has 3 times as many books as Lucille. How many books does Javier have? _____

22. Cho's father is 48 years old. Cho is $\frac{1}{6}$ as old as her father. How old is Cho? _____

Name _____   **Date** _____

Going Further

Copyright © Houghton Mifflin Company. All rights reserved.

▶Use a Venn Diagram to Show Relationships

A **multiple** is the product of a number and any other number.

For example, 6, 12, 18, and 24 are multiples of 6.

Find the rule that was used for sorting the data. Then label the Venn diagram.

1.

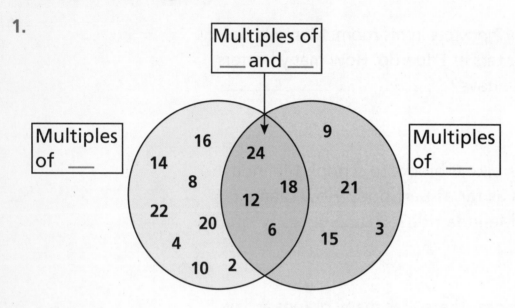

Multiples of ___ and ___

Multiples of ___

Multiples of ___

16 14 24 9 8 18 21 22 12 20 6 15 3 4 10 2

2.

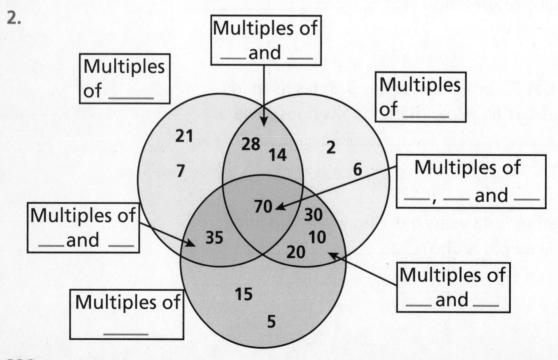

Multiples of ___ and ___

Multiples of ___

Multiples of ___

Multiples of ___, ___ and ___

Multiples of ___ and ___

Multiples of ___ and ___

Multiples of ___

21 28 14 2 7 6 70 30 35 10 20 15 5

Comparison Word Problems

Class Activity

Name _____ **Date** _____

▶ **Use Comparison Bars**

Draw comparison bars to help you solve each problem.

Jadzia's dog Roscoe competes in dog shows. He has won 42 blue ribbons and 6 red ribbons.

1. Roscoe has won _____ as many blue ribbons as red ribbons.

2. Roscoe has won _____ as many red ribbons as blue ribbons.

Daphne is 7 years old. Her grandfather is 56 years old.

3. Daphne is _____ as old as her grandfather.

4. Daphne's grandfather is _____ as old as Daphne.

Beatrice has 48 dolls. Cathy has 8 dolls.

5. Beatrice has _____ as many dolls as Cathy.

6. Cathy has _____ as many dolls as Beatrice.

Make a drawing to help you solve each problem.

7. Last month Elle earned $8 helping her aunt with chores. This month she earned 4 times as much by doing yard work for her neighbor. How much did Elle earn this month?

_____

8. Minh picked 48 peaches. His little brother Bao picked $\frac{1}{8}$ as many peaches as Minh. How many peaches did Bao pick?

_____

9. Carlos has 49 music CDs. His cousin Luisa has $\frac{1}{7}$ as many music CDs as Carlos. How many CDs does Luisa have?

_____

10. Rose rode the roller coaster 6 times. Leila rode the roller coaster 3 times as many times as Rose. How many times did Leila ride the roller coaster?

_____

More Comparison Word Problems

Class Activity

Name _____   Date _____

►Use a Bar Graph to Compare

Shannon collects souvenir T-shirts from the places she visits. She made this bar graph to show the colors of the shirts in her collection.

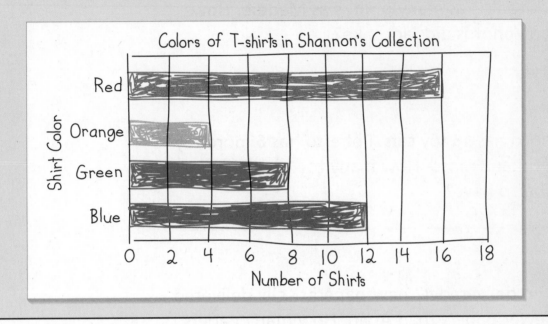

11. Shannon has _____ as many red shirts as green shirts.

    Shannon has _____ as many green shirts as red shirts.

12. Shannon has _____ as many red shirts as orange shirts.

    Shannon has _____ as many orange shirts as red shirts.

13. Shannon has _____ as many blue shirts as orange shirts.

    Shannon has _____ as many orange shirts as blue shirts.

14. Shannon has _____ as many orange shirts as green shirts.

    Shannon has _____ as many green shirts as orange shirts.

▶Solve Comparison Problems

Solve.

15. Maddie took 21 photographs on her vacation. Jack took $\frac{1}{3}$ as many photos as Maddie. How many photos did Jack take?

_____

16. Franco has 18 toy cars. Roberto has 6 more toy cars than Franco. How many toy cars does Roberto have?

_____

17. Arvin delivered 42 newspapers. Kelly delivered 7 fewer papers than Arvin. How many papers did Kelly deliver?

_____

18. Jasmine's dog weighs 8 pounds. Shaunda's dog weighs 5 times as much as Jasmine's dog. How much does Shaunda's dog weigh?

_____

19. Charles is $\frac{1}{4}$ as old as his father. His father is 36 years old. How old is Charles?

_____

More Comparison Word Problems

▶Sprints for 8s

As your teacher reads each multiplication or division, write your answer in the space provided.

× 8	÷ 8
a. _____	a. _____
b. _____	b. _____
c. _____	c. _____
d. _____	d. _____
e. _____	e. _____
f. _____	f. _____
g. _____	g. _____
h. _____	h. _____
i. _____	i. _____
j. _____	j. _____

►Check Sheet 9: 7s and Squares

7s Multiplications	7s Divisions	Squares Multiplications	Squares Divisions
$4 \times 7 = 28$	$14 / 7 = 2$	$8 \times 8 = 64$	$81 / 9 = 9$
$7 \cdot 2 = 14$	$28 \div 7 = 4$	$10 \cdot 10 = 100$	$4 \div 2 = 2$
$7 * 8 = 56$	$70 / 7 = 10$	$3 * 3 = 9$	$25 / 5 = 5$
$7 \times 7 = 49$	$56 \div 7 = 8$	$9 \times 9 = 81$	$1 \div 1 = 1$
$7 \cdot 1 = 7$	$42 / 7 = 6$	$4 \cdot 4 = 16$	$100 / 10 = 10$
$7 * 10 = 70$	$63 \div 7 = 9$	$7 * 7 = 49$	$36 \div 6 = 6$
$3 \times 7 = 21$	$7 / 7 = 1$	$5 \times 5 = 25$	$49 / 7 = 7$
$7 \cdot 6 = 42$	$49 \div 7 = 7$	$6 \cdot 6 = 36$	$9 \div 3 = 3$
$5 * 7 = 35$	$21 / 7 = 3$	$1 * 1 = 1$	$64 / 8 = 8$
$7 \times 9 = 63$	$35 / 7 = 5$	$5 * 5 = 25$	$16 / 4 = 4$
$7 \cdot 4 = 28$	$7 \div 7 = 1$	$1 \cdot 1 = 1$	$100 \div 10 = 10$
$9 * 7 = 63$	$63 / 7 = 9$	$3 \cdot 3 = 9$	$49 / 7 = 7$
$2 \times 7 = 14$	$14 \div 7 = 2$	$10 \times 10 = 100$	$1 \div 1 = 1$
$7 \cdot 5 = 35$	$70 / 7 = 10$	$4 \times 4 = 16$	$9 / 3 = 3$
$8 * 7 = 56$	$21 \div 7 = 3$	$9 * 9 = 81$	$64 \div 8 = 8$
$7 \times 3 = 21$	$49 / 7 = 7$	$2 \times 2 = 4$	$4 / 2 = 2$
$6 \cdot 7 = 42$	$28 \div 7 = 4$	$6 * 6 = 36$	$81 \div 9 = 9$
$10 * 7 = 70$	$56 \div 7 = 8$	$7 \times 7 = 49$	$16 \div 4 = 4$
$1 \times 7 = 7$	$35 / 7 = 5$	$5 \cdot 5 = 25$	$25 / 5 = 5$
$7 \cdot 7 = 49$	$42 \div 7 = 6$	$8 \cdot 8 = 64$	$36 \div 6 = 6$

Name _____ **Date** _____

Class Activity

▶ Explore Square Numbers

Write an equation to show the area of each large square.

1. $1 \times 1 = 1$ 2. _____   3. _____   4. _____

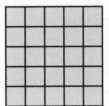 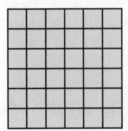

5. _____   6. _____

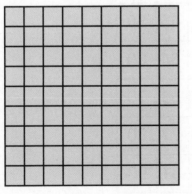 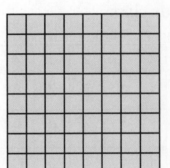

7. _____   8. _____

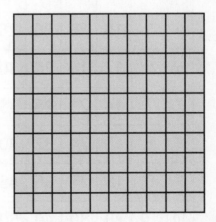

9. _____   10. _____

Name

Date

Class Activity

▶Look for Patterns

11. List the products in exercises 1–10 in order. Discuss the patterns you see with your class.

The numbers you listed in exercise 11 are called **square numbers** because they are the areas of squares with whole-number lengths of sides. A square number is the product of a whole number and itself. So, if *n* is a whole number, *n* × *n* is a square number.

▶Patterns on the Multiplication Table

12. In the table below, circle the products that are square numbers. Discuss the patterns you see with your class.

X	1	2	3	4	5	6	7	8	9	10
1	1	2	3	4	5	6	7	8	9	10
2	2	4	6	8	10	12	14	16	18	20
3	3	6	9	12	15	18	21	24	27	30
4	4	8	12	16	20	24	28	32	36	40
5	5	10	15	20	25	30	35	40	45	50
6	6	12	18	24	30	36	42	48	54	60
7	7	14	21	28	35	42	49	56	63	70
8	8	16	24	32	40	48	56	64	72	80
9	9	18	27	36	45	54	63	72	81	90
10	10	20	30	40	50	60	70	80	90	100

Square Numbers

▶Check Sheet 10: 6s, 7s, and 8s

6s, 7s, and 8s Multiplications	6s, 7s, and 8s Multiplications	6s, 7s, and 8s Divisions	6s, 7s, and 8s Divisions
1 × 6 = 6	0 × 8 = 0	24 / 6 = 4	54 / 6 = 9
6 • 7 = 42	6 • 2 = 12	21 ÷ 7 = 3	24 ÷ 8 = 3
3 * 8 = 24	4 * 7 = 28	16 / 8 = 2	14 / 7 = 2
6 × 2 = 12	8 × 3 = 24	24 ÷ 8 = 3	32 ÷ 8 = 4
7 • 5 = 35	5 • 6 = 30	14 / 7 = 2	18 / 6 = 3
8 * 4 = 32	7 * 2 = 14	30 ÷ 6 = 5	56 ÷ 7 = 8
6 × 6 = 36	3 × 8 = 24	35 / 7 = 5	40 / 8 = 5
8 • 7 = 56	6 • 4 = 24	24 ÷ 8 = 3	35 ÷ 7 = 5
9 * 8 = 72	0 * 7 = 0	18 / 6 = 3	12 / 6 = 2
6 × 10 = 60	8 × 1 = 8	12 / 6 = 2	21 / 7 = 3
7 • 1 = 7	8 • 6 = 48	42 ÷ 7 = 6	16 ÷ 8 = 2
8 * 3 = 24	7 * 9 = 63	56 / 8 = 7	42 / 6 = 7
5 × 6 = 30	10 × 8 = 80	49 ÷ 7 = 7	80 ÷ 8 = 10
4 • 7 = 28	6 • 10 = 60	16 / 8 = 2	36 / 6 = 6
2 * 8 = 16	3 * 7 = 21	60 ÷ 6 = 10	7 ÷ 7 = 1
7 × 7 = 49	8 × 4 = 32	54 / 6 = 9	64 / 8 = 8
7 • 6 = 42	6 • 5 = 30	8 ÷ 8 = 1	24 ÷ 6 = 4
8 * 8 = 64	7 * 4 = 28	28 ÷ 7 = 4	21 ÷ 7 = 3
9 × 6 = 54	8 × 8 = 64	72 / 8 = 9	49 / 7 = 7
10 • 7 = 70	6 • 9 = 54	56 ÷ 7 = 8	24 ÷ 8 = 3

▶ **Check Sheet 11: 0s–10s**

0s–10s Multiplications	0s–10s Multiplications	0s–10s Divisions	0s–10s Divisions
$9 \times 0 = 0$	$9 \times 4 = 36$	$9 / 1 = 9$	$90 / 10 = 9$
$1 \cdot 1 = 1$	$5 \cdot 9 = 45$	$12 \div 3 = 4$	$64 \div 8 = 8$
$2 * 3 = 6$	$6 * 10 = 60$	$14 / 2 = 7$	$15 / 5 = 3$
$1 \times 3 = 3$	$7 \times 3 = 21$	$20 \div 4 = 5$	$12 \div 6 = 2$
$5 \cdot 4 = 20$	$5 \cdot 3 = 15$	$10 / 5 = 2$	$14 / 7 = 2$
$7 * 5 = 35$	$4 * 1 = 4$	$48 \div 8 = 6$	$45 \div 9 = 5$
$6 \times 9 = 54$	$7 \times 5 = 35$	$35 / 7 = 5$	$8 / 1 = 8$
$0 \cdot 7 = 0$	$6 \cdot 3 = 18$	$60 \div 6 = 10$	$30 \div 3 = 10$
$1 * 8 = 8$	$8 * 7 = 56$	$81 / 9 = 9$	$16 / 4 = 4$
$9 \times 8 = 72$	$5 \times 8 = 40$	$20 / 10 = 2$	$8 / 2 = 4$
$2 \cdot 10 = 20$	$9 \cdot 9 = 81$	$16 \div 2 = 8$	$80 \div 10 = 8$
$0 * 7 = 0$	$9 * 10 = 90$	$30 / 5 = 6$	$36 / 4 = 9$
$4 \times 1 = 4$	$0 \times 0 = 0$	$49 \div 7 = 7$	$25 \div 5 = 5$
$2 \cdot 4 = 8$	$1 \cdot 0 = 0$	$60 / 6 = 10$	$42 / 7 = 6$
$10 * 3 = 30$	$1 * 6 = 6$	$30 \div 3 = 10$	$36 \div 6 = 6$
$8 \times 4 = 32$	$7 \times 2 = 14$	$8 / 1 = 8$	$90 / 9 = 10$
$5 \cdot 8 = 40$	$6 \cdot 3 = 18$	$16 \div 4 = 4$	$24 \div 8 = 3$
$4 * 6 = 24$	$4 * 5 = 20$	$16 \div 8 = 2$	$6 \div 2 = 3$
$7 \times 0 = 0$	$6 \times 6 = 36$	$40 / 10 = 4$	$9 / 3 = 3$
$1 \cdot 8 = 8$	$10 \cdot 7 = 70$	$36 \div 9 = 4$	$1 \div 1 = 1$

▶Dashes 9–12

Complete each Dash. Check your answers on page 339.

Dash 9 2s, 3s, 4s, 5s, 9s Multiplications	Dash 10 2s, 3s, 4s, 5s, 9s Divisions	Dash 11 6s, 7s, 8s Multiplications	Dash 12 6s, 7s, 8s Divisions
a. $6 \times 3 =$ ___	a. $16 / 4 =$ ___	a. $7 \times 7 =$ ___	a. $21 / 7 =$ ___
b. $4 \cdot 7 =$ ___	b. $54 \div 9 =$ ___	b. $6 \cdot 3 =$ ___	b. $16 \div 8 =$ ___
c. $8 * 2 =$ ___	c. $4 / 2 =$ ___	c. $8 * 6 =$ ___	c. $54 / 6 =$ ___
d. $5 \times 3 =$ ___	d. $28 \div 4 =$ ___	d. $6 \times 6 =$ ___	d. $48 \div 8 =$ ___
e. $4 \cdot 4 =$ ___	e. $25 / 5 =$ ___	e. $7 \cdot 6 =$ ___	e. $64 / 8 =$ ___
f. $3 * 9 =$ ___	f. $21 \div 3 =$ ___	f. $4 * 7 =$ ___	f. $42 \div 6 =$ ___
g. $9 \times 9 =$ ___	g. $40 / 4 =$ ___	g. $9 \times 7 =$ ___	g. $56 / 7 =$ ___
h. $8 \cdot 9 =$ ___	h. $81 \div 9 =$ ___	h. $6 \cdot 9 =$ ___	h. $72 \div 8 =$ ___
i. $6 * 4 =$ ___	i. $35 / 5 =$ ___	i. $6 * 4 =$ ___	i. $18 / 6 =$ ___
j. $3 \times 3 =$ ___	j. $12 / 3 =$ ___	j. $8 \times 8 =$ ___	j. $28 / 7 =$ ___
k. $2 \cdot 7 =$ ___	k. $2 \div 2 =$ ___	k. $7 \cdot 3 =$ ___	k. $56 \div 8 =$ ___
l. $8 * 5 =$ ___	l. $63 / 9 =$ ___	l. $8 * 7 =$ ___	l. $30 / 6 =$ ___
m. $4 \times 9 =$ ___	m. $36 \div 4 =$ ___	m. $6 \times 7 =$ ___	m. $63 \div 7 =$ ___
n. $9 \cdot 5 =$ ___	n. $18 / 2 =$ ___	n. $3 \cdot 6 =$ ___	n. $32 / 8 =$ ___
o. $7 * 3 =$ ___	o. $9 \div 3 =$ ___	o. $2 * 7 =$ ___	o. $48 \div 6 =$ ___
p. $2 \times 2 =$ ___	p. $36 / 9 =$ ___	p. $9 \times 8 =$ ___	p. $49 / 7 =$ ___
q. $8 \cdot 4 =$ ___	q. $40 \div 5 =$ ___	q. $5 \cdot 6 =$ ___	q. $36 \div 6 =$ ___
r. $5 * 1 =$ ___	r. $12 \div 4 =$ ___	r. $7 * 8 =$ ___	r. $24 \div 8 =$ ___
s. $5 \times 5 =$ ___	s. $9 / 9 =$ ___	s. $3 \times 7 =$ ___	s. $42 / 7 =$ ___
t. $6 \cdot 9 =$ ___	t. $14 \div 2 =$ ___	t. $9 \cdot 6 =$ ___	t. $24 \div 6 =$ ___

► Dashes 9–12

Complete each Dash. Check your answers on page 339.

Dash 9 2s, 3s, 4s, 5s, 9s Multiplications	Dash 10 2s, 3s, 4s, 5s, 9s Divisions	Dash 11 6s, 7s, 8s Multiplications	Dash 12 6s, 7s, 8s Divisions
a. $6 \times 3 =$ ___	a. $16 / 4 =$ ___	a. $7 \times 7 =$ ___	a. $21 / 7 =$ ___
b. $4 \cdot 7 =$ ___	b. $54 \div 9 =$ ___	b. $6 \cdot 3 =$ ___	b. $16 \div 8 =$ ___
c. $8 * 2 =$ ___	c. $4 / 2 =$ ___	c. $8 * 6 =$ ___	c. $54 / 6 =$ ___
d. $5 \times 3 =$ ___	d. $28 \div 4 =$ ___	d. $6 \times 6 =$ ___	d. $48 \div 8 =$ ___
e. $4 \cdot 4 =$ ___	e. $25 / 5 =$ ___	e. $7 \cdot 6 =$ ___	e. $64 / 8 =$ ___
f. $3 * 9 =$ ___	f. $21 \div 3 =$ ___	f. $4 * 7 =$ ___	f. $42 \div 6 =$ ___
g. $9 \times 9 =$ ___	g. $40 / 4 =$ ___	g. $9 \times 7 =$ ___	g. $56 / 7 =$ ___
h. $8 \cdot 9 =$ ___	h. $81 \div 9 =$ ___	h. $6 \cdot 9 =$ ___	h. $72 \div 8 =$ ___
i. $6 * 4 =$ ___	i. $35 / 5 =$ ___	i. $6 * 4 =$ ___	i. $18 / 6 =$ ___
j. $3 \times 3 =$ ___	j. $12 / 3 =$ ___	j. $8 \times 8 =$ ___	j. $28 / 7 =$ ___
k. $2 \cdot 7 =$ ___	k. $2 \div 2 =$ ___	k. $7 \cdot 3 =$ ___	k. $56 \div 8 =$ ___
l. $8 * 5 =$ ___	l. $63 / 9 =$ ___	l. $8 * 7 =$ ___	l. $30 / 6 =$ ___
m. $4 \times 9 =$ ___	m. $36 \div 4 =$ ___	m. $6 \times 7 =$ ___	m. $63 \div 7 =$ ___
n. $9 \cdot 5 =$ ___	n. $18 / 2 =$ ___	n. $3 \cdot 6 =$ ___	n. $32 / 8 =$ ___
o. $7 * 3 =$ ___	o. $9 \div 3 =$ ___	o. $2 * 7 =$ ___	o. $48 \div 6 =$ ___
p. $2 \times 2 =$ ___	p. $36 / 9 =$ ___	p. $9 \times 8 =$ ___	p. $49 / 7 =$ ___
q. $8 \cdot 4 =$ ___	q. $40 \div 5 =$ ___	q. $5 \cdot 6 =$ ___	q. $36 \div 6 =$ ___
r. $5 * 1 =$ ___	r. $12 \div 4 =$ ___	r. $7 * 8 =$ ___	r. $24 \div 8 =$ ___
s. $5 \times 5 =$ ___	s. $9 / 9 =$ ___	s. $3 \times 7 =$ ___	s. $42 / 7 =$ ___
t. $6 \cdot 9 =$ ___	t. $14 \div 2 =$ ___	t. $9 \cdot 6 =$ ___	t. $24 \div 6 =$ ___

▶Answers to Dashes 9–12

Use this sheet to check your answers to the dashes on page 337.

Dash 9 2s, 3s, 4s, 5s, 9s Multiplications	Dash 10 2s, 3s, 4s, 5s, 9s Divisions	Dash 11 6s, 7s, 8s Multiplications	Dash 12 6s, 7s, 8s Divisions
a. $6 \times 3 = 18$	a. $16 / 4 = 4$	a. $7 \times 7 = 49$	a. $21 / 7 = 3$
b. $4 \cdot 7 = 28$	b. $54 \div 9 = 6$	b. $6 \cdot 3 = 18$	b. $16 \div 8 = 2$
c. $8 * 2 = 16$	c. $4 / 2 = 2$	c. $8 * 6 = 48$	c. $54 / 6 = 9$
d. $5 \times 3 = 15$	d. $28 \div 4 = 7$	d. $6 \times 6 = 36$	d. $48 \div 8 = 6$
e. $4 \cdot 4 = 16$	e. $25 / 5 = 5$	e. $7 \cdot 6 = 42$	e. $64 / 8 = 8$
f. $3 * 9 = 27$	f. $21 \div 3 = 7$	f. $4 * 7 = 28$	f. $42 \div 6 = 7$
g. $9 \times 9 = 81$	g. $40 / 4 = 10$	g. $9 \times 7 = 63$	g. $56 / 7 = 8$
h. $8 \cdot 9 = 72$	h. $81 \div 9 = 9$	h. $6 \cdot 9 = 54$	h. $72 \div 8 = 9$
i. $6 * 4 = 24$	i. $35 / 5 = 7$	i. $6 * 4 = 24$	i. $18 / 6 = 3$
j. $3 \times 3 = 9$	j. $12 / 3 = 4$	j. $8 \times 8 = 64$	j. $28 / 7 = 4$
k. $2 \cdot 7 = 14$	k. $2 \div 2 = 1$	k. $7 \cdot 3 = 21$	k. $56 \div 8 = 7$
l. $8 * 5 = 40$	l. $63 / 9 = 7$	l. $8 * 7 = 56$	l. $30 / 6 = 5$
m. $4 \times 9 = 36$	m. $36 \div 4 = 9$	m. $6 \times 7 = 42$	m. $63 \div 7 = 9$
n. $9 \cdot 5 = 45$	n. $18 / 2 = 9$	n. $3 \cdot 6 = 18$	n. $32 / 8 = 4$
o. $7 * 3 = 21$	o. $9 \div 3 = 3$	o. $2 * 7 = 14$	o. $48 \div 6 = 8$
p. $2 \times 2 = 4$	p. $36 / 9 = 4$	p. $9 \times 8 = 72$	p. $49 / 7 = 7$
q. $8 \cdot 4 = 32$	q. $40 \div 5 = 8$	q. $5 \cdot 6 = 30$	q. $36 \div 6 = 6$
r. $5 * 1 = 5$	r. $12 \div 4 = 3$	r. $7 * 8 = 56$	r. $24 \div 8 = 3$
s. $5 \times 5 = 25$	s. $9 / 9 = 1$	s. $3 \times 7 = 21$	s. $42 / 7 = 6$
t. $6 \cdot 9 = 54$	t. $14 \div 2 = 7$	t. $9 \cdot 6 = 54$	t. $24 \div 6 = 4$

Answers to Dashes 9–12

Class Activity

| Name | Date |

► Play *High Card Wins*

Read the rules for playing *High Card Wins*. Then play the game with your partner.

Rules for *High Card Wins*

Number of players: 2
What you will need: 1 set of multiplication Strategy Cards *or* 1 set of division Strategy Cards

1. Shuffle the cards. Then deal all the cards evenly between the two players.

2. Players put their stacks in front of them, problem side up.

3. Each player takes the top card from his or her stack and puts it problem side up in the center of the table.

4. Each player says the answer (product or quotient) and then turns the card over to check. Then do one of the following:
   - If one player says the wrong answer, the other player takes both cards and puts them at the bottom of his or her pile.
   - If both players say the wrong answer, both players take back their cards and put them at the bottom of their piles.
   - If both players say the correct answer, the player with the higher product takes both cards and puts them at the bottom of his or her pile. If the answers are the same, the players set the cards aside and play another round. The winner of the next round takes all the cards.

5. When time is up, the player with the most cards wins.

Play *High Card Wins* **341**

Play *High Card Wins*

Name _____ **Date** _____

▶Multiply and Divide with 11 and 12

What patterns do you see?

× 11	÷ 11
1 × 11 = 11	11 ÷ 11 = 1
2 × 11 = 22	22 ÷ 11 = 2
3 × 11 = 33	33 ÷ 11 = 3
4 × 11 = 44	44 ÷ 11 = 4
5 × 11 = 55	55 ÷ 11 = 5
6 × 11 = 66	66 ÷ 11 = 6
7 × 11 = 77	77 ÷ 11 = 7
8 × 11 = 88	88 ÷ 11 = 8
9 × 11 = 99	99 ÷ 11 = 9
10 × 11 = 110	110 ÷ 11 = 10

× 12	÷ 12
1 × 12 = 12	12 ÷ 12 = 1
2 × 12 = 24	24 ÷ 12 = 2
3 × 12 = 36	36 ÷ 12 = 3
4 × 12 = 48	48 ÷ 12 = 4
5 × 12 = 60	60 ÷ 12 = 5
6 × 12 = 72	72 ÷ 12 = 6
7 × 12 = 84	84 ÷ 12 = 7
8 × 12 = 96	96 ÷ 12 = 8
9 × 12 = 108	108 ÷ 12 = 9
10 × 12 = 120	120 ÷ 12 = 10

▶11s and 12s Multiplication Table

Complete the multiplication table.

You can use multiplications you know to help.

$8 \times 12 = 8 \times (5 + 7)$
$\qquad = (8 \times 5) + (8 \times 7)$
$\qquad = 40 + 56$
$\qquad = 96$
$\quad$ or
$8 \times 12 = 8 \times (10 + 2)$
$\qquad = (8 \times 10) + (8 \times 2)$
$\qquad = 80 + 16$
$\qquad = 96$

X	1	2	3	4	5	6	7	8	9	10	11	12
1	1	2	3	4	5	6	7	8	9	10		
2	2	4	6	8	10	12	14	16	18	20		
3	3	6	9	12	15	18	21	24	27	30		
4	4	8	12	16	20	24	28	32	36	40		
5	5	10	15	20	25	30	35	40	45	50		
6	6	12	18	24	30	36	42	48	54	60		
7	7	14	21	28	35	42	49	56	63	70		
8	8	16	24	32	40	48	56	64	72	80		
9	9	18	27	36	45	54	63	72	81	90		
10	10	20	30	40	50	60	70	80	90	100		
11												
12												

Practice with 6s, 7s, and 8s

Class Activity

Name _____ Date _____

▶ Sprints for 7s

As your teacher reads each multiplication or division, write your answer in the space provided.

× 7	÷ 7
a. _____	a. _____
b. _____	b. _____
c. _____	c. _____
d. _____	d. _____
e. _____	e. _____
f. _____	f. _____
g. _____	g. _____
h. _____	h. _____
i. _____	i. _____
j. _____	j. _____

▶ Choose the Operation

Solve.

1. Ernie helped his mother work in the yard for 3 days. He earned $6 each day. How much did he earn in all?

   _____

2. Ernie helped his mother work in the yard for 3 days. He earned $6 the first day, $5 the second day, and $7 the third day. How much did he earn in all?

   _____

3. Troy had $18. He gave $6 to each of his brothers and had no money left. How many brothers does Troy have?

   _____

4. Troy gave $18 to his brothers. He gave $4 to Raj, $7 to Darnell, and the rest to Jai. How much money did Jai get?

   _____

5. Jinja has 4 cousins. Grant has 7 more cousins than Jinja. How many cousins does Grant have?

   _____

6. Jinja has 4 cousins. Grant has 7 times as many cousins as Jinja. How many cousins does Grant have?

   _____

7. Camille has 15 fewer books than Jane has. Camille has 12 books. How many does Jane have?

   _____

8. Camille has half as many books as Jane has. Camille has 15 books. How many books does Jane have?

   _____

Class Activity

Name _____ Date _____

▶ Write an Equation

Write an equation to solve each problem.

Show your work.

9. Luke had a $5 bill. He spent $3.73 on a sandwich. How much change did he get?

_____

10. Ramona is putting tiles on the kitchen floor. She will lay 8 rows of tiles, with 7 tiles in each row. How many tiles will Ramona use?

_____

11. Josh earned As on 6 tests last year. Jenna earned As on 6 times as many tests. How many As did Jenna earn?

_____

12. Sophie bought a stuffed animal for $2.76 and a board game for $6.99. How much money did Sophie spend?

_____

13. The Duarte family has 15 pets. Each of the 3 Duarte children care for the same number of pets. How many pets does each child care for?

_____

14. Ahmed spent $9 on CD. Zal paid $6 more for the same CD at a different store. How much did Zal spend on the CD?

_____

▶ Write the Question

Write a question for the given information and solve.

15. Anna read 383 pages this month. Chris read 416 pages.

    Question: _____

    Solution: _____

16. Marisol had 128 beads in her jewelry box. She gave away 56 of them.

    Question: _____

    Solution: _____

17. Louis put 72 marbles in 8 bags. He put the same number of marbles in each bag.

    Question: _____

    Solution: _____

18. Geoff planted 4 pots of seeds. He planted 6 seeds in each pot.

    Question: _____

    Solution: _____

19. Last week, Marly read for 2 hours. Jamal read for 7 times as many hours as Marly did.

    Question: _____

    Solution: _____

Solve Mixed Word Problems

▶ Write the Problem

Write a problem that can be solved using the given equation. Then solve.

20. $9 \times 6 = \square$ Solution: _____

_____

_____

_____

21. $324 - 176 = \square$ Solution: _____

_____

_____

_____

22. $56 \div 7 = \square$ Solution: _____

_____

_____

_____

23. $459 + 635 = \square$ Solution: _____

_____

_____

_____

24. **Math Journal** Choose an operation. Write a word problem that involves that operation. Write an equation to solve your word problem.

Going Further

▶ Solve Open-Ended Problems

Back to School Sale!

Pencils – 4 for $1.00

Markers – $2.95 per box

Notebooks – $1.19 each

Calculators – $3.00 each

Pens – 60¢ each

Backpacks – $9.00 each

Crayons – $2.59 per box

1. Hilda has $20.00 to buy her school supplies. She needs 12 pencils, 2 pens, a box of crayons, and a backpack. She also needs either a box of markers or a calculator, but not both. How should Hilda spend her $20.00 to get everything she needs and still have money left over? Explain your thinking.

Party Favors on Sale!

6 for $1 Party Bags

Bubbles 4 for $1

3 for $2 Funny Glasses

6 for $2 Crazy Straws

4 for $3 High-Bounce Balls

Yo-Yo's 6 for $4

2. Ivan and his dad are planning to make 12 identical party bags with 3 different items in each bag for a total cost under $25.00. List the 3 items they should buy. Explain your thinking.

3. **Math Journal** Find another combination of toys that Ivan and his dad could buy.

Solve Mixed Word Problems

▶ Use Order of Operations

> This exercise involves subtraction and multiplication:
>
> $$10 - 3 \times 2$$

1. What do you get if you subtract first and then multiply? _____

2. What do you get if you multiply first and then subtract? _____

> To make sure everyone has the same answer to problems like this one, people have decided that multiplication and division will be done *before* addition and subtraction. The answer you found in question 2 is correct.
>
> If you want to tell people to add or subtract first, you must use parentheses. Parentheses mean "Do this first." For example, if you want people to subtract first in the exercise above, write it like this:
>
> $$(10 - 3) \times 2$$

Find the answer.

3. $5 + 4 \times 2 =$ _____

4. $(9 - 3) \times 6 =$ _____

5. $8 \div 2 + 2 =$ _____

6. $6 \times (8 - 1) =$ _____

Rewrite each statement, using symbols and numbers instead of words.

7. Add 4 and 3, and multiply the total by 8. _____

8. Multiply 3 by 8, and add 4 to the total. _____

Class Activity

▶ Multi-Step Problems

Solve each problem.

Show your work.

9. A roller coaster has 7 cars. Each car has 4 seats. If there were 3 empty seats, how many people were on the roller coaster?

_____

10. Each week, Marta earns $10 babysitting. She always spends $3 and saves the rest. How much does she save in 8 weeks?

_____

11. Abu bought 6 packs of stickers. Each pack had 8 stickers. Then Abu's friend gave him 10 more stickers. How many stickers does Abu have now?

_____

12. Zoe made some snacks. She put 4 apple slices and 2 melon slices on each plate. She prepared 5 plates. How many slices of fruit did Zoe use in all?

_____

13. Kyle ordered 8 pizzas for his party. Each pizza was cut into 8 slices. 48 of the slices were plain cheese, and the rest had mushrooms. How many slices of pizza had mushrooms?

_____

14. Nadia counted 77 birds on the pond. 53 were ducks, and the rest were geese. Then the geese flew away in 4 equal flocks. How many geese were in each flock?

_____

▶ More Multi-Step Problems

Solve each problem. Draw a picture if you need to.   *Show your work.*

15. Lakesha has filled two pages of her stamp book. Both pages have 5 rows of stamps. On one page, there are 5 stamps in each row. On the opposite page, there are 3 stamps in each row. How many stamps are on the two pages?

   _____

16. Kagami baked 86 blueberry muffins. Her sisters ate 5 of them. Kagami divided the remaining muffins equally among 9 plates. How many muffins did she put on each plate?

   _____

17. Lucia had 42 plums. Jorge had 12 more plums than Lucia. Jorge divided his plums equally among 6 people. How many plums did each person get?

   _____

18. Dana arranged her books on 5 shelves, with 8 books on each shelf. Hassan arranged his books on 4 shelves, with 9 books on each shelf. Who has more books? How many more?

   _____

19. Juana has 21 shirts. Leslie had one third as many shirts as Juana, but then she bought 4 more. How many shirts does Leslie have now?

   _____

Name _____ **Date** _____

Going Further

▶ Multiply 2- and 3-Digit Numbers by 1-Digit Numbers

There are 26 cars in the water ride at Smiley Park. Each car can fit 7 people. How many people in all can fit in the cars of the water ride?

$26 \times 7 = \square$

The Expanded Notation Method

$$26 = 20 + 6$$
$$\times\ 7 = \quad \times 7$$
$$\overline{}$$
$$6 \times 7 = \qquad 42$$
$$20 \times 7 = \quad +140$$
$$\overline{\qquad\quad 182}$$

You can multiply by the ones first.

$$346 = 300 + 40 + 6$$
$$\times\ 2 = \qquad\qquad 2$$
$$\overline{}$$
$$2 \times 300 = \quad 600$$
$$2 \times\ 40 = \qquad 80$$
$$2 \times\quad 6 = \quad +\ 12$$
$$\overline{\qquad\quad 692}$$

The Rectangle Sections Method

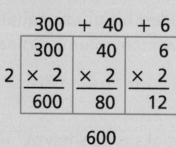

$$
\begin{array}{c}
7 \\
\times\ 20 \\
\hline
140
\end{array}
\qquad
\begin{array}{c}
140 \\
+\ 42 \\
\hline
182
\end{array}
$$

$$
\begin{array}{c}
7 \\
\times\ 6 \\
\hline
42
\end{array}
$$

$$
\begin{array}{c|c|c}
300 & 40 & 6 \\
\times\ 2 & \times\ 2 & \times\ 2 \\
\hline
600 & 80 & 12
\end{array}
$$

$$
\begin{array}{r}
600 \\
80 \\
+\ 12 \\
\hline
692
\end{array}
$$

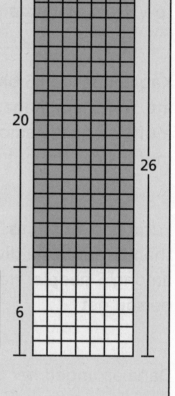

Multiply.

1. $\begin{array}{r} 14 \\ \times\ 4 \\ \hline \end{array}$

2. $\begin{array}{r} 78 \\ \times\ 8 \\ \hline \end{array}$

3. $\begin{array}{r} 86 \\ \times\ 6 \\ \hline \end{array}$

4. $\begin{array}{r} 325 \\ \times\ 3 \\ \hline \end{array}$

5. $\begin{array}{r} 497 \\ \times\ 2 \\ \hline \end{array}$

6. $\begin{array}{r} 637 \\ \times\ 5 \\ \hline \end{array}$

Solve Multi-Step Word Problems

▶Dashes 13–16

Complete each Dash. Check your answers on page 357.

Dash 13 2s, 3s, 4s, 5s, 9s Multiplications	Dash 14 2s, 3s, 4s, 5s, 9s Divisions	Dash 15 6s, 7s, 8s Multiplications	Dash 16 6s, 7s, 8s Divisions
a. 7 × 4 = ___	a. 9 / 3 = ___	a. 8 × 8 = ___	a. 72 / 8 = ___
b. 5 • 5 = ___	b. 45 ÷ 9 = ___	b. 9 • 6 = ___	b. 49 ÷ 7 = ___
c. 2 * 9 = ___	c. 81 / 9 = ___	c. 7 * 6 = ___	c. 35 / 7 = ___
d. 3 × 8 = ___	d. 36 ÷ 4 = ___	d. 5 × 7 = ___	d. 64 ÷ 8 = ___
e. 4 • 4 = ___	e. 20 / 5 = ___	e. 3 • 8 = ___	e. 14 / 7 = ___
f. 5 * 9 = ___	f. 16 ÷ 4 = ___	f. 8 * 6 = ___	f. 18 ÷ 6 = ___
g. 6 × 3 = ___	g. 12 / 2 = ___	g. 6 × 3 = ___	g. 64 / 8 = ___
h. 7 • 2 = ___	h. 54 ÷ 9 = ___	h. 7 • 7 = ___	h. 48 ÷ 6 = ___
i. 9 * 9 = ___	i. 15 / 3 = ___	i. 4 * 8 = ___	i. 8 / 8 = ___
j. 6 × 4 = ___	j. 27 / 3 = ___	j. 6 × 6 = ___	j. 56 / 7 = ___
k. 2 • 2 = ___	k. 18 ÷ 2 = ___	k. 4 • 6 = ___	k. 32 ÷ 8 = ___
l. 5 * 3 = ___	l. 28 / 4 = ___	l. 7 * 9 = ___	l. 63 / 7 = ___
m. 4 × 8 = ___	m. 40 ÷ 5 = ___	m. 5 × 6 = ___	m. 30 ÷ 6 = ___
n. 3 • 3 = ___	n. 45 / 5 = ___	n. 4 • 7 = ___	n. 56 / 8 = ___
o. 7 * 5 = ___	o. 4 ÷ 2 = ___	o. 8 * 2 = ___	o. 72 ÷ 8 = ___
p. 8 × 5 = ___	p. 9 / 3 = ___	p. 1 × 6 = ___	p. 36 / 6 = ___
q. 4 • 3 = ___	q. 32 ÷ 4 = ___	q. 2 • 7 = ___	q. 40 ÷ 8 = ___
r. 2 * 8 = ___	r. 63 ÷ 9 = ___	r. 8 * 5 = ___	r. 21 ÷ 7 = ___
s. 9 × 4 = ___	s. 15 / 3 = ___	s. 8 × 1 = ___	s. 42 / 6 = ___
t. 6 • 9 = ___	t. 24 ÷ 4 = ___	t. 9 • 8 = ___	t. 7 ÷ 7 = ___

▶Dashes 13–16

Complete each Dash. Check your answers on page 357.

Dash 13 2s, 3s, 4s, 5s, 9s Multiplications	Dash 14 2s, 3s, 4s, 5s, 9s Divisions	Dash 15 6s, 7s, 8s Multiplications	Dash 16 6s, 7s, 8s Divisions
a. $7 \times 4 =$ ___	a. $9 / 3 =$ ___	a. $8 \times 8 =$ ___	a. $72 / 8 =$ ___
b. $5 \cdot 5 =$ ___	b. $45 \div 9 =$ ___	b. $9 \cdot 6 =$ ___	b. $49 \div 7 =$ ___
c. $2 * 9 =$ ___	c. $81 / 9 =$ ___	c. $7 * 6 =$ ___	c. $35 / 7 =$ ___
d. $3 \times 8 =$ ___	d. $36 \div 4 =$ ___	d. $5 \times 7 =$ ___	d. $64 \div 8 =$ ___
e. $4 \cdot 4 =$ ___	e. $20 / 5 =$ ___	e. $3 \cdot 8 =$ ___	e. $14 / 7 =$ ___
f. $5 * 9 =$ ___	f. $16 \div 4 =$ ___	f. $8 * 6 =$ ___	f. $18 \div 6 =$ ___
g. $6 \times 3 =$ ___	g. $12 / 2 =$ ___	g. $6 \times 3 =$ ___	g. $64 / 8 =$ ___
h. $7 \cdot 2 =$ ___	h. $54 \div 9 =$ ___	h. $7 \cdot 7 =$ ___	h. $48 \div 6 =$ ___
i. $9 * 9 =$ ___	i. $15 / 3 =$ ___	i. $4 * 8 =$ ___	i. $8 / 8 =$ ___
j. $6 \times 4 =$ ___	j. $27 / 3 =$ ___	j. $6 \times 6 =$ ___	j. $56 / 7 =$ ___
k. $2 \cdot 2 =$ ___	k. $18 \div 2 =$ ___	k. $4 \cdot 6 =$ ___	k. $32 \div 8 =$ ___
l. $5 * 3 =$ ___	l. $28 / 4 =$ ___	l. $7 * 9 =$ ___	l. $63 / 7 =$ ___
m. $4 \times 8 =$ ___	m. $40 \div 5 =$ ___	m. $5 \times 6 =$ ___	m. $30 \div 6 =$ ___
n. $3 \cdot 3 =$ ___	n. $45 / 5 =$ ___	n. $4 \cdot 7 =$ ___	n. $56 / 8 =$ ___
o. $7 * 5 =$ ___	o. $4 \div 2 =$ ___	o. $8 * 2 =$ ___	o. $72 \div 8 =$ ___
p. $8 \times 5 =$ ___	p. $9 / 3 =$ ___	p. $1 \times 6 =$ ___	p. $36 / 6 =$ ___
q. $4 \cdot 3 =$ ___	q. $32 \div 4 =$ ___	q. $2 \cdot 7 =$ ___	q. $40 \div 8 =$ ___
r. $2 * 8 =$ ___	r. $63 \div 9 =$ ___	r. $8 * 5 =$ ___	r. $21 \div 7 =$ ___
s. $9 \times 4 =$ ___	s. $15 / 3 =$ ___	s. $8 \times 1 =$ ___	s. $42 / 6 =$ ___
t. $6 \cdot 9 =$ ___	t. $24 \div 4 =$ ___	t. $9 \cdot 8 =$ ___	t. $7 \div 7 =$ ___

▶Answers to Dashes 13–16

Use this sheet to check your answers to the dashes
on page 355.

Dash 13 2s, 3s, 4s, 5s, 9s Multiplications	Dash 14 2s, 3s, 4s, 5s, 9s Divisions	Dash 15 6s, 7s, 8s Multiplications	Dash 16 6s, 7s, 8s Divisions
a. $7 \times 4 = 28$	a. $9 / 3 = 3$	a. $8 \times 8 = 64$	a. $72 / 8 = 9$
b. $5 \cdot 5 = 25$	b. $45 \div 9 = 5$	b. $9 \cdot 6 = 54$	b. $49 \div 7 = 7$
c. $2 * 9 = 18$	c. $81 / 9 = 9$	c. $7 * 6 = 42$	c. $35 / 7 = 5$
d. $3 \times 8 = 24$	d. $36 \div 4 = 9$	d. $5 \times 7 = 35$	d. $64 \div 8 = 8$
e. $4 \cdot 4 = 16$	e. $20 / 5 = 4$	e. $3 \cdot 8 = 24$	e. $14 / 7 = 2$
f. $5 * 9 = 45$	f. $16 \div 4 = 4$	f. $8 * 6 = 48$	f. $18 \div 6 = 3$
g. $6 \times 3 = 18$	g. $12 / 2 = 6$	g. $6 \times 3 = 18$	g. $64 / 8 = 8$
h. $7 \cdot 2 = 14$	h. $54 \div 9 = 6$	h. $7 \cdot 7 = 49$	h. $48 \div 6 = 8$
i. $9 * 9 = 81$	i. $15 / 3 = 5$	i. $4 * 8 = 32$	i. $8 / 8 = 1$
j. $6 \times 4 = 24$	j. $27 / 3 = 9$	j. $6 \times 6 = 36$	j. $56 / 7 = 8$
k. $2 \cdot 2 = 4$	k. $18 \div 2 = 9$	k. $4 \cdot 6 = 24$	k. $32 \div 8 = 4$
l. $5 * 3 = 15$	l. $28 / 4 = 7$	l. $7 * 9 = 63$	l. $63 / 7 = 9$
m. $4 \times 8 = 32$	m. $40 \div 5 = 8$	m. $5 \times 6 = 30$	m. $30 \div 6 = 5$
n. $3 \cdot 3 = 9$	n. $45 / 5 = 9$	n. $4 \cdot 7 = 28$	n. $56 / 8 = 7$
o. $7 * 5 = 35$	o. $4 \div 2 = 2$	o. $8 * 2 = 16$	o. $72 \div 8 = 9$
p. $8 \times 5 = 40$	p. $9 / 3 = 3$	p. $1 \times 6 = 6$	p. $36 / 6 = 6$
q. $4 \cdot 3 = 12$	q. $32 \div 4 = 8$	q. $2 \cdot 7 = 14$	q. $40 \div 8 = 5$
r. $2 * 8 = 16$	r. $63 \div 9 = 7$	r. $8 * 5 = 40$	r. $21 \div 7 = 3$
s. $9 \times 4 = 36$	s. $15 / 3 = 5$	s. $8 \times 1 = 8$	s. $42 / 6 = 7$
t. $6 \cdot 9 = 54$	t. $24 \div 4 = 6$	t. $9 \cdot 8 = 72$	t. $7 \div 7 = 1$

Answers to Dashes 13–16

►Complex Multi-Step Word Problems

Solve.

1. A farm had 413 chickens. Then 9 of the hens laid 6 eggs each. All of the eggs have hatched except 3. How many chickens does the farm have now?

_____

2. There are 8 houses on Jeremiah's street. Each house has 1 willow tree, 6 apple trees, and 2 olive trees. How many trees are on Jeremiah's street in all?

_____

3. Tim has 6 marbles. Adrian has twice as many marbles as Tim. Ryan has 3 fewer marbles than Adrian. Leslie has 5 times as many marbles as Ryan. How many marbles does Leslie have?

_____

4. Allen has 548 baseball cards. Drew has 362 more cards than Allen. Lacy has 76 fewer baseball cards than Drew. How many more baseball cards does Lacy have than Allen?

_____

5. Angela had $4.00. She bought 3 gumballs for 9¢ each and 2 apples for 63¢ each. How much money does Angela have now?

_____

6. Jasmine has $40. Ahmad has half as much money. Ahmad wants to buy an action figure for $5.76 and a backpack for $14.89. Does Ahmad have enough money?

_____

▶ More Complex Word Problems

Solve. Show your work on another sheet of paper.

7. Mr. Marconi made 9 pizzas. He divided the pizzas into 3 equal groups. One group was pizzas with mushrooms, one group had peppers, and one group was plain cheese. He cut each pizza into 8 slices. How many slices had either mushrooms or peppers?

8. Kelsey wants to see all 700 paintings in the art museum. Last week she saw 473 of them. Today she visited 9 more rooms in the museum. There are 8 paintings in each room. How many paintings does Kelsey still have to see?

9. The Nelson Notebook Company makes 3 kinds of wire spirals for their notebooks.

   Each type of spiral comes in 3 colors. The table gives information about all 9 spirals the company makes.

   Which spiral colors are tight, which are medium, and which are loose? How do you know?

Tight   Medium   Loose

Color	Length of Wire Before Spiral	Length of Spiral
Blue	18 in.	9 in.
Red	20 in.	10 in.
Black	21 in.	7 in.
Green	24 in.	6 in.
White	26 in.	13 in.
Orange	27 in.	9 in.
Silver	28 in.	7 in.
Purple	33 in.	11 in.
Gold	40 in.	10 in.

▶Dashes 17–20

Complete each Dash. Check your answers on page 363.

Dash 17 All Factors Multiplications	Dash 18 All Factors Divisions	Dash 19 All Factors Multiplications	Dash 20 All Factors Divisions
a. $5 \times 4 =$ ___	a. $100 / 10 =$ ___	a. $4 \times 5 =$ ___	a. $81 / 9 =$ ___
b. $8 \cdot 10 =$ ___	b. $36 \div 4 =$ ___	b. $8 \cdot 8 =$ ___	b. $21 \div 7 =$ ___
c. $6 * 6 =$ ___	c. $56 / 7 =$ ___	c. $6 * 1 =$ ___	c. $30 / 6 =$ ___
d. $9 \times 2 =$ ___	d. $14 \div 2 =$ ___	d. $6 \times 7 =$ ___	d. $42 \div 6 =$ ___
e. $7 \cdot 7 =$ ___	e. $32 / 8 =$ ___	e. $9 \cdot 3 =$ ___	e. $15 / 3 =$ ___
f. $3 * 8 =$ ___	f. $36 \div 6 =$ ___	f. $7 * 8 =$ ___	f. $72 \div 8 =$ ___
g. $8 \times 9 =$ ___	g. $40 / 5 =$ ___	g. $10 \times 7 =$ ___	g. $28 / 4 =$ ___
h. $4 \cdot 1 =$ ___	h. $64 \div 8 =$ ___	h. $6 \cdot 0 =$ ___	h. $48 \div 8 =$ ___
i. $2 * 2 =$ ___	i. $5 / 1 =$ ___	i. $4 * 4 =$ ___	i. $49 / 7 =$ ___
j. $8 \times 7 =$ ___	j. $21 / 3 =$ ___	j. $7 \times 5 =$ ___	j. $18 / 2 =$ ___
k. $5 \cdot 5 =$ ___	k. $48 \div 6 =$ ___	k. $6 \cdot 4 =$ ___	k. $63 \div 9 =$ ___
l. $7 * 6 =$ ___	l. $42 / 7 =$ ___	l. $9 * 7 =$ ___	l. $54 / 9 =$ ___
m. $4 \times 8 =$ ___	m. $5 \div 5 =$ ___	m. $2 \times 6 =$ ___	m. $20 \div 10 =$ ___
n. $9 \cdot 4 =$ ___	n. $72 / 9 =$ ___	n. $4 \cdot 7 =$ ___	n. $24 / 4 =$ ___
o. $9 * 9 =$ ___	o. $54 \div 6 =$ ___	o. $9 * 6 =$ ___	o. $56 \div 8 =$ ___
p. $10 \times 3 =$ ___	p. $18 / 6 =$ ___	p. $6 \times 3 =$ ___	p. $60 / 6 =$ ___
q. $6 \cdot 8 =$ ___	q. $60 \div 6 =$ ___	q. $3 \cdot 3 =$ ___	q. $36 \div 9 =$ ___
r. $5 * 9 =$ ___	r. $63 \div 7 =$ ___	r. $10 * 10 =$ ___	r. $20 \div 4 =$ ___
s. $6 \times 9 =$ ___	s. $16 / 4 =$ ___	s. $8 \times 2 =$ ___	s. $45 / 5 =$ ___
t. $0 \cdot 1 =$ ___	t. $24 \div 6 =$ ___	t. $5 \cdot 9 =$ ___	t. $28 \div 7 =$ ___

▶Dashes 17–20

Complete each Dash. Check your answers on page 363.

Dash 17 All Factors Multiplications	Dash 18 All Factors Divisions	Dash 19 All Factors Multiplications	Dash 20 All Factors Divisions
a. $5 \times 4 =$ ___	a. $100 / 10 =$ ___	a. $4 \times 5 =$ ___	a. $81 / 9 =$ ___
b. $8 \cdot 10 =$ ___	b. $36 \div 4 =$ ___	b. $8 \cdot 8 =$ ___	b. $21 \div 7 =$ ___
c. $6 * 6 =$ ___	c. $56 / 7 =$ ___	c. $6 * 1 =$ ___	c. $30 / 6 =$ ___
d. $9 \times 2 =$ ___	d. $14 \div 2 =$ ___	d. $6 \times 7 =$ ___	d. $42 \div 6 =$ ___
e. $7 \cdot 7 =$ ___	e. $32 / 8 =$ ___	e. $9 \cdot 3 =$ ___	e. $15 / 3 =$ ___
f. $3 * 8 =$ ___	f. $36 \div 6 =$ ___	f. $7 * 8 =$ ___	f. $72 \div 8 =$ ___
g. $8 \times 9 =$ ___	g. $40 / 5 =$ ___	g. $10 \times 7 =$ ___	g. $28 / 4 =$ ___
h. $4 \cdot 1 =$ ___	h. $64 \div 8 =$ ___	h. $6 \cdot 0 =$ ___	h. $48 \div 8 =$ ___
i. $2 * 2 =$ ___	i. $5 / 1 =$ ___	i. $4 * 4 =$ ___	i. $49 / 7 =$ ___
j. $8 \times 7 =$ ___	j. $21 / 3 =$ ___	j. $7 \times 5 =$ ___	j. $18 / 2 =$ ___
k. $5 \cdot 5 =$ ___	k. $48 \div 6 =$ ___	k. $6 \cdot 4 =$ ___	k. $63 \div 9 =$ ___
l. $7 * 6 =$ ___	l. $42 / 7 =$ ___	l. $9 * 7 =$ ___	l. $54 / 9 =$ ___
m. $4 \times 8 =$ ___	m. $5 \div 5 =$ ___	m. $2 \times 6 =$ ___	m. $20 \div 10 =$ ___
n. $9 \cdot 4 =$ ___	n. $72 / 9 =$ ___	n. $4 \cdot 7 =$ ___	n. $24 / 4 =$ ___
o. $9 * 9 =$ ___	o. $54 \div 6 =$ ___	o. $9 * 6 =$ ___	o. $56 \div 8 =$ ___
p. $10 \times 3 =$ ___	p. $18 / 6 =$ ___	p. $6 \times 3 =$ ___	p. $60 / 6 =$ ___
q. $6 \cdot 8 =$ ___	q. $60 \div 6 =$ ___	q. $3 \cdot 3 =$ ___	q. $36 \div 9 =$ ___
r. $5 * 9 =$ ___	r. $63 \div 7 =$ ___	r. $10 * 10 =$ ___	r. $20 \div 4 =$ ___
s. $6 \times 9 =$ ___	s. $16 / 4 =$ ___	s. $8 \times 2 =$ ___	s. $45 / 5 =$ ___
t. $0 \cdot 1 =$ ___	t. $24 \div 6 =$ ___	t. $5 \cdot 9 =$ ___	t. $28 \div 7 =$ ___

▶Answers to Dashes 17–20

Use this sheet to check your answers to the dashes
on page 361.

Dash 17 All Factors Multiplications	Dash 18 All Factors Divisions	Dash 19 All Factors Multiplications	Dash 20 All Factors Divisions
a. $5 \times 4 = 20$	a. $100 / 10 = 10$	a. $4 \times 5 = 20$	a. $81 / 9 = 9$
b. $8 \cdot 10 = 80$	b. $36 \div 4 = 9$	b. $8 \cdot 8 = 64$	b. $21 \div 7 = 3$
c. $6 * 6 = 36$	c. $56 / 7 = 8$	c. $6 * 1 = 6$	c. $30 / 6 = 5$
d. $9 \times 2 = 18$	d. $14 \div 2 = 7$	d. $6 \times 7 = 42$	d. $42 \div 6 = 7$
e. $7 \cdot 7 = 49$	e. $32 / 8 = 4$	e. $9 \cdot 3 = 27$	e. $15 / 3 = 5$
f. $3 * 8 = 24$	f. $36 \div 6 = 6$	f. $7 * 8 = 56$	f. $72 \div 8 = 9$
g. $8 \times 9 = 72$	g. $40 / 5 = 8$	g. $10 \times 7 = 70$	g. $28 / 4 = 7$
h. $4 \cdot 1 = 4$	h. $64 \div 8 = 8$	h. $6 \cdot 0 = 0$	h. $48 \div 8 = 6$
i. $2 * 2 = 4$	i. $5 / 1 = 5$	i. $4 * 4 = 16$	i. $49 / 7 = 7$
j. $8 \times 7 = 56$	j. $21 / 3 = 7$	j. $7 \times 5 = 35$	j. $18 / 2 = 9$
k. $5 \cdot 5 = 25$	k. $48 \div 6 = 8$	k. $6 \cdot 4 = 24$	k. $63 \div 9 = 7$
l. $7 * 6 = 42$	l. $42 / 7 = 6$	l. $9 * 7 = 63$	l. $54 / 9 = 6$
m. $4 \times 8 = 32$	m. $5 \div 5 = 1$	m. $2 \times 6 = 12$	m. $20 \div 10 = 2$
n. $9 \cdot 4 = 36$	n. $72 / 9 = 8$	n. $4 \cdot 7 = 28$	n. $24 / 4 = 6$
o. $9 * 9 = 81$	o. $54 \div 6 = 9$	o. $9 * 6 = 54$	o. $56 \div 8 = 7$
p. $10 \times 3 = 30$	p. $18 / 6 = 3$	p. $6 \times 3 = 18$	p. $60 / 6 = 10$
q. $6 \cdot 8 = 48$	q. $60 \div 6 = 10$	q. $3 \cdot 3 = 9$	q. $36 \div 9 = 4$
r. $5 * 9 = 45$	r. $63 \div 7 = 9$	r. $10 * 10 = 100$	r. $20 \div 4 = 5$
s. $6 \times 9 = 54$	s. $16 / 4 = 4$	s. $8 \times 2 = 16$	s. $45 / 5 = 9$
t. $0 \cdot 1 = 0$	t. $24 \div 6 = 4$	t. $5 \cdot 9 = 45$	t. $28 \div 7 = 4$

Answers to Dashes 17–20

▶ Solve Multi-Step Word Problems

Solve.

Show your work.

1. Raul spent 8 minutes doing his homework. His older sister spent 5 minutes less than 7 times as many minutes doing her homework. How many minutes did Raul's sister spend on her homework?

   _____

2. At Sonya's cello recital, there were 8 rows of chairs, with 6 chairs in each row. There was a person in each chair, and there were 17 more people standing. How many people were in the audience altogether?

   _____

3. Tova's art teacher asked her to cut out construction paper squares with an area of 36 square centimeters each. What should the side lengths of the squares be?

   _____

4. Mukesh was making 7 salads. He opened a can of olives and put 6 olives on each salad. Then he ate the rest of the olives in the can. If there were 51 olives to start with, how many olives did Mukesh eat?

   _____

5. Peter wallpapered a wall that was 8 feet wide and 9 feet high. He had 28 square feet of wallpaper left over. How many square feet of wallpaper did he start with?

   _____

Name _____ Date _____

Class Activity

►What's My Rule?

A **function table** is a table of ordered pairs. For every input number, there is only one output number. The rule describes what to do to the input number to get the output number.

Write the rule and then complete the function table.

6.
Rule: _____

Input	Output
7	42
8	____
____	54
6	36

7.
Rule: _____

Input	Output
81	9
45	5
72	____
____	7

8.
Rule: _____

Input	Output
4	28
8	56
6	____
7	____

9.
Rule: _____

Input	Output
32	8
8	2
____	3
24	____

10.
Rule: _____

Input	Output
21	7
27	9
____	6
15	____

11.
Rule: _____

Input	Output
5	25
____	40
9	____
3	15

Play Multiplication and Division Games

▶ Play *Division Three-in-a-Row*

Rules for *Division Three-in-a-Row*

Number of players: 2
What You Will Need: Division Strategy Cards, one *Three-in-a-Row* Game Grid for each player

1. Each player writes any nine quotients in the squares of a game grid. A player may write the same quotient more than once.

2. Shuffle the cards. Place them division side up in the center of the table.

3. Players take turns. On each turn, a player completes the division on the top card and then turns the card over to check the answer.

4. For a correct answer, if the quotient is on the game grid, the player puts an X through that grid square. If the answer is wrong, or if the quotient is not on the grid, the player doesn't mark anything. The player puts the card division side up on the bottom of the stack.

5. The first player to mark three squares in a row (horizontally, vertically, or diagonally) wins.

Play *Division Three-in-a-Row*

▶ **Math and Social Studies**

Every state has a state bird.

- The meadowlark is the state bird of 6 states.
- The robin is the state bird of half of the number of states that have the meadowlark as a state bird.
- The wren is the state bird of 1 fewer states than the states with the robin as state bird.
- The bluebird is the state bird of twice the number of states with the wren as state bird.

1. On a piece of grid paper, make a graph that shows the data about state birds above.

2. Put the birds in order from most often used as a state bird to least often used as a state bird.

   _____

3. The number of states with a cardinal as state bird is one more than the number of states with the meadowlark as the state bird. How many states have the cardinal as state bird?

   _____

4. Write a word problem about the data in the graph and give the answer. Trade problems with a partner and solve.

   _____

Name _____ **Date** _____

Class Activity

▶ **Street Chalk Art Fair**

Around the country cities block off streets and hold Chalk Art Fairs. Each person or group is given a rectangle outlined on the street for their chalk painting.

5. One of the rectangles on the street has a perimeter of 12 feet. Each side of the rectangle is a whole number of feet. What is the greatest area it could have? Explain.

_____
_____
_____
_____
_____
_____

6. One of the rectangles has a perimeter of 16 feet. Each side of the rectangle is a whole number of feet. What is the smallest area it could have? Explain.

_____
_____
_____
_____
_____
_____
_____

7. Lupe and her friends have their choice of a rectangle that is 9 feet by 2 feet or a rectangle that is 4 feet by 5 feet. They want to choose the rectangle with the greatest area. Which rectangle should they choose? Explain.

_____
_____
_____
_____

8. Which of the rectangles described in Problem 7 should Lupe and her friends choose if they want the rectangle with the greatest perimeter? Explain.

_____
_____
_____
_____

Use Mathematical Processes

Basic Multiplications

1. $8 \times 9 =$ ___　　2. $1 * 10 =$ ___　　3. $3 \bullet 5 =$ ___　　4. $2 * 8 =$ ___

5. $5 * 3 =$ ___　　6. $0 \times 7 =$ ___　　7. $8 \times 8 =$ ___　　8. $2 * 7 =$ ___

9. $4 \bullet 10 =$ ___　　10. $7 \bullet 2 =$ ___　　11. $3 \bullet 8 =$ ___　　12. $7 * 10 =$ ___

13. $4 \bullet 4 =$ ___　　14. $1 * 3 =$ ___　　15. $0 \times 0 =$ ___　　16. $4 * 9 =$ ___

17. $10 \bullet 6 =$ ___　　18. $1 \times 5 =$ ___　　19. $7 \bullet 5 =$ ___　　20. $2 \bullet 6 =$ ___

21. $5 \times 8 =$ ___　　22. $4 * 5 =$ ___　　23. $6 \bullet 8 =$ ___　　24. $0 \times 3 =$ ___

25. $9 * 9 =$ ___　　26. $9 * 2 =$ ___　　27. $0 \times 10 =$ ___　　28. $0 \times 2 =$ ___

29. $7 * 8 =$ ___　　30. $8 \bullet 7 =$ ___　　31. $1 \bullet 7 =$ ___　　32. $1 \times 9 =$ ___

33. $2 * 9 =$ ___　　34. $6 \bullet 10 =$ ___　　35. $5 \times 9 =$ ___　　36. $5 \times 5 =$ ___

37. $2 * 3 =$ ___　　38. $3 \bullet 2 =$ ___　　39. $3 \times 4 =$ ___　　40. $0 * 4 =$ ___

41. $9 \times 10 =$ ___　　42. $3 \times 6 =$ ___　　43. $0 \times 6 =$ ___　　44. $9 \times 6 =$ ___

45. $6 \times 7 =$ ___　　46. $10 \times 10 =$ ___　　47. $8 \times 3 =$ ___　　48. $6 \times 2 =$ ___

49. $10 \times 5 =$ ___　　50. $6 \times 4 =$ ___

Basic Multiplications

51. $1 * 0 =$ ___   52. $8 \cdot 2 =$ ___   53. $10 * 7 =$ ___   54. $1 * 2 =$ ___

55. $5 * 2 =$ ___   56. $9 \cdot 7 =$ ___   57. $8 \times 5 =$ ___   58. $6 \cdot 6 =$ ___

59. $7 \cdot 9 =$ ___   60. $1 * 1 =$ ___   61. $7 * 3 =$ ___   62. $0 * 9 =$ ___

63. $4 * 2 =$ ___   64. $10 \times 8 =$ ___   65. $2 \cdot 4 =$ ___   66. $4 \cdot 8 =$ ___

67. $2 * 2 =$ ___   68. $1 * 4 =$ ___   69. $1 \times 6 =$ ___   70. $0 \cdot 1 =$ ___

71. $5 \cdot 10 =$ ___   72. $3 \cdot 10 =$ ___   73. $0 \cdot 8 =$ ___   74. $7 * 4 =$ ___

75. $9 * 3 =$ ___   76. $4 \times 3 =$ ___   77. $6 \times 9 =$ ___   78. $7 * 6 =$ ___

79. $3 \cdot 7 =$ ___   80. $2 \cdot 10 =$ ___   81. $8 * 4 =$ ___   82. $9 * 8 =$ ___

83. $6 \cdot 3 =$ ___   84. $5 \times 6 =$ ___   85. $3 * 9 =$ ___   86. $9 \cdot 5 =$ ___

87. $1 \times 8 =$ ___   88. $8 \times 10 =$ ___   89. $2 \times 5 =$ ___   90. $5 \times 4 =$ ___

91. $0 \times 5 =$ ___   92. $10 \times 9 =$ ___   93. $4 \times 7 =$ ___   94. $7 \times 7 =$ ___

95. $6 \times 5 =$ ___   96. $9 \times 4 =$ ___   97. $4 \times 6 =$ ___   98. $5 \times 7 =$ ___

99. $8 \times 6 =$ ___   100. $3 \times 3 =$ ___

Basic Divisions

1. 6 / 3 = ___   2. 40 / 8 = ___   3. 10 ÷ 1 = ___   4. 40 ÷ 10 = ___

5. 32 / 8 = ___   6. 2 ÷ 2 = ___   7. 80 ÷ 10 = ___   8. 4 ÷ 1 = ___

9. 16 ÷ 2 = ___   10. 30 / 6 = ___   11. 90 / 10 = ___   12. 24 ÷ 6 = ___

13. 4 / 2 = ___   14. 8 / 4 = ___   15. 9 / 9 = ___   16. 6 ÷ 1 = ___

17. 24 ÷ 3 = ___   18. 81 / 9 = ___   19. 15 ÷ 5 = ___   20. 7 ÷ 7 = ___

21. 12 ÷ 6 = ___   22. 20 / 10 = ___   23. 35 ÷ 7 = ___   24. 72 / 9 = ___

25. $7\overline{)28}$ 26. $9\overline{)27}$ 27. $3\overline{)3}$ 28. $7\overline{)49}$

29. $3\overline{)27}$ 30. $3\overline{)15}$ 31. $4\overline{)28}$ 32. $8\overline{)16}$

33. $1\overline{)2}$ 34. $5\overline{)45}$ 35. $5\overline{)10}$ 36. $8\overline{)72}$

37. $10\overline{)70}$ 38. $5\overline{)5}$ 39. $7\overline{)70}$ 40. $6\overline{)18}$

41. $\frac{56}{7}$ = ___   42. $\frac{48}{8}$ = ___   43. $\frac{21}{7}$ = ___   44. $\frac{36}{4}$ = ___

45. $\frac{3}{1}$ = ___   46. $\frac{42}{6}$ = ___   47. $\frac{18}{3}$ = ___   48. $\frac{30}{3}$ = ___

49. $\frac{45}{9}$ = ___   50. $\frac{16}{4}$ = ___

Basic Divisions

51. $6 \div 6 =$ ___ 52. $42 / 7 =$ ___ 53. $20 \div 5 =$ ___ 54. $90 / 9 =$ ___

55. $36 / 9 =$ ___ 56. $35 \div 5 =$ ___ 57. $1 / 1 =$ ___ 58. $50 \div 10 =$ ___

59. $54 / 9 =$ ___ 60. $12 \div 2 =$ ___ 61. $10 \div 2 =$ ___ 62. $24 / 8 =$ ___

63. $14 \div 7 =$ ___ 64. $12 \div 3 =$ ___ 65. $63 / 7 =$ ___ 66. $4 \div 4 =$ ___

67. $6 / 2 =$ ___ 68. $25 \div 5 =$ ___ 69. $5 \div 1 =$ ___ 70. $7 \div 1 =$ ___

71. $60 / 10 =$ ___ 72. $18 \div 2 =$ ___ 73. $60 / 6 =$ ___ 74. $9 / 3 =$ ___

75. $5\overline{)50}$ 76. $10\overline{)10}$ 77. $4\overline{)12}$ 78. $8\overline{)80}$

79. $5\overline{)30}$ 80. $8\overline{)56}$ 81. $6\overline{)54}$ 82. $9\overline{)63}$

83. $4\overline{)24}$ 84. $8\overline{)8}$ 85. $8\overline{)64}$ 86. $1\overline{)7}$

87. $2\overline{)8}$ 88. $10\overline{)30}$ 89. $4\overline{)40}$ 90. $6\overline{)48}$

91. $\frac{32}{4} =$ ___ 92. $\frac{9}{1} =$ ___ 93. $\frac{36}{6} =$ ___ 94. $\frac{100}{10} =$ ___

95. $\frac{14}{2} =$ ___ 96. $\frac{21}{3} =$ ___ 97. $\frac{40}{5} =$ ___ 98. $\frac{20}{4} =$ ___

99. $\frac{20}{2} =$ ___ 100. $\frac{18}{9} =$ ___

Basic Divisions Test

Multiply or divide.

1. $7 \times 8 =$ ☐

2. $6 \bullet 9 =$ ☐

3. $55 \div 1 =$ ☐

4. $72 \div 9 =$ ☐

5. $30 \times 0 =$ ☐

6. $49 / 7 =$ ☐

7. $4 \bullet 3 =$ ☐

8. $2 * 10 =$ ☐

9. $3 \times 9 =$ ☐

10. ☐ $6)\overline{24}$

11. ☐ $7)\overline{28}$

12. ☐ $9)\overline{45}$

Solve.

Show your work.

13. Lucinda collected 4 eggs from the chicken house. Mark collected 32 eggs. How many times as many eggs did Mark collect than Lucinda?

_____

14. Carrie found 7 seashells at the beach. Her brother found 4 times as many. How many seashells did her brother find?

_____

15. The supermarket sells small boxes of cereal in packages of 8. Mrs. Smith bought 6 packages. How many boxes of cereal did she buy?

_____

16. The area of Keshawn's garden is 36 square feet. Its width is 4 feet. What is the length of his garden?

_____

Write an equation to solve the problem.

17. A class has 35 goldfish and 5 fish bowls. How many fish will be in each bowl if the same number of fish are in each bowl?

_____

Solve.

18. Mr. Howell arranged 56 books on 8 shelves with the same number on each shelf. How many books were on each shelf?

_____

19. Mr. Alberto has 48 students to divide into teams of 8. Mr. Yates has 81 students to divide into teams of 9. How many more teams does Mr. Yates have than Mr. Alberto?

_____

20. **Extended Response** Marcie has 7 bean bag dolls. Lucy has 3 times as many dolls as Marcie. Janice has twice as many dolls as Marcie and Lucy combined. How many more dolls does Janice have than Marcie? Explain the steps you used to solve the problem.

_____

_____

_____

_____

_____

_____

▶ Make an Analog Clock

Attach the clock hands to the clock face using a prong fastener.

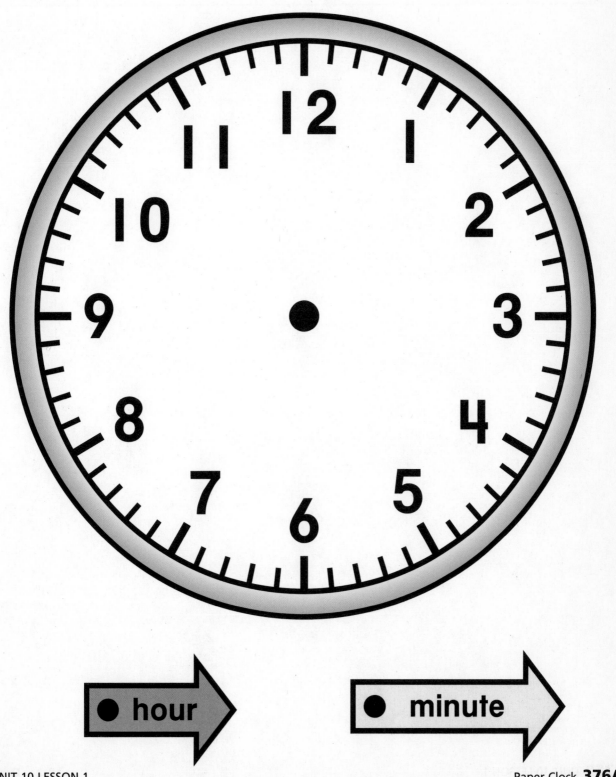

Paper Clock

▶Time to 5 Minutes

Write the time on the digital clock. Then write how to say the time.

20.

```
    :
```

_____

21.

```
    :
```

_____

22.

```
    :
```

_____

23.

```
    :
```

_____

Write the time on the digital clock.

24. ten minutes after eight
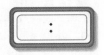

25. seven twenty-five

26. eleven fifty

▶Time to 1 Minute

Write the time on the digital clock. Then write how to say the time.

27.

```
    :
```

_____

28.

```
    :
```

_____

29.

```
    :
```

_____

30.

```
    :
```

_____

Write the time on the digital clock.

31. ten fourteen

32. fifty-two minutes after eight

33. seven twenty-eight

▶Times Before and After the Hour

Write the time as minutes *after* an hour and minutes *before* an hour.

34.

_____

_____

35.

_____

_____

36.

_____

_____

37.

_____

_____

38.

_____

_____

39.

_____

_____

40.

_____

_____

41.

_____

_____

42.

_____

_____

Dear Family,

In math class, your child is beginning a unit about time. This topic is directly connected to home and community and involves skills your child will use often in everyday situations.

Students are reading time to the hour, half-hour, quarter-hour, five minutes, and minute, as well as describing the time before the hour and after the hour.

For example, you can read 3:49 both as after and before the hour.

Forty-nine minutes after three

Eleven minutes before four

Students use calendars and clocks to find elapsed time and to solve problems involving elapsed time in days, weeks, months, hours, and minutes.

At the end of the unit, students will link the movement of the minute hand around a clock to angle measures in degrees. They will divide the 360° rotation of a circle by 60 minutes to find that each minute on a clock represents a 6° rotation. They will use this fact to solve word problems involving elapsed time, problems which give them practice multiplying and dividing by 6.

Help your child read time and find elapsed time. Ask your child to estimate how long it takes to do activities such as eating a meal, traveling to the store, or doing homework. Have your child look at the clock when starting an activity and then again at the end of the activity. Ask how long the activity took.

Talk to your child about events that will be happening over the next year and ask how many days or months there are until those events. Talk about past events in the year and ask your child how many days or months it has been since those events happened.

If you have any questions or comments, please call or write to me.

Sincerely,
Your child's teacher

Estimada familia:

En la clase de matemáticas su niño empieza una unidad sobre la hora. Este tema se relaciona directamente con la casa y la comunidad, y trata de destrezas que su niño usará a menudo en situaciones de la vida diaria.

Los estudiantes leen la hora, la media hora, el cuarto de hora, cinco minutos y un minuto; también describen la hora antes y después de la hora en punto.

Por ejemplo, se puede leer 3:49 de dos maneras:

Las tres y cuarenta y nueve

Las cuatro menos once

Los estudiantes usan calendarios y relojes para hallar el tiempo transcurrido y para resolver problemas de tiempo transcurrido en días, semanas, meses, horas y minutos.

Al final de la unidad, los estudiantes harán la conexión entre el movimiento del minutero del reloj y las medidas de ángulos en grados. Dividirán la rotación de 360° de un círculo entre 60 minutos para hallar que cada minuto del reloj representa una rotación de 6°. Luego usarán este dato para resolver problemas verbales que tratan de tiempo transcurrido, lo que a su vez les deja practicar la multiplicación y la división por 6.

Ayude a su niño a leer la hora y hallar el tiempo transcurrido. Pídale que estime cuánto le lleva hacer actividades como comer, una comida, ir a la tienda o hacer la tarea. Pídale que se fije en la hora antes de empezar una actividad y luego otra vez al completar la actividad. Pídale que le diga cuánto tiempo le llevó hacer la actividad.

Háblele a su niño acerca de sucesos que ocurrirán durante el año que viene y pregúntele cuántos días o meses faltan para que sucedan. Háblele de sucesos pasados del año y pregúntele cuántos días o meses hace que pasaron estos sucesos.

Si tiene alguna pregunta o comentario, por favor comuníquese conmigo.

Atentamente,
El maestro de su niño

►Features of Calendars

January

Sun	Mon	Tues	Wed	Thurs	Fri	Sat
	1	2	3	4	5	6
7	8	9	10	11	12	13
14	15	16	17	18	19	20
21	22	23	24	25	26	27
28	29	30	31			

February

Sun	Mon	Tues	Wed	Thurs	Fri	Sat
				1	2	3
4	5	6	7	8	9	10
11	12	13	14	15	16	17
18	19	20	21	22	23	24
25	26	27	28			

March

Sun	Mon	Tues	Wed	Thurs	Fri	Sat
				1	2	3
4	5	6	7	8	9	10
11	12	13	14	15	16	17
18	19	20	21	22	23	24
25	26	27	28	29	30	31

April

Sun	Mon	Tues	Wed	Thurs	Fri	Sat
1	2	3	4	5	6	7
8	9	10	11	12	13	14
15	16	17	18	19	20	21
22	23	24	25	26	27	28
29	30					

May

Sun	Mon	Tues	Wed	Thurs	Fri	Sat
		1	2	3	4	5
6	7	8	9	10	11	12
13	14	15	16	17	18	19
20	21	22	23	24	25	26
27	28	29	30	31		

June

Sun	Mon	Tues	Wed	Thurs	Fri	Sat
					1	2
3	4	5	6	7	8	9
10	11	12	13	14	15	16
17	18	19	20	21	22	23
24	25	26	27	28	29	30

Class Activity

July

Sun	Mon	Tues	Wed	Thurs	Fri	Sat
1	2	3	4	5	6	7
8	9	10	11	12	13	14
15	16	17	18	19	20	21
22	23	24	25	26	27	28
29	30	31				

August

Sun	Mon	Tues	Wed	Thurs	Fri	Sat
			1	2	3	4
5	6	7	8	9	10	11
12	13	14	15	16	17	18
19	20	21	22	23	24	25
26	27	28	29	30	31	

September

Sun	Mon	Tues	Wed	Thurs	Fri	Sat
						1
2	3	4	5	6	7	8
9	10	11	12	13	14	15
16	17	18	19	20	21	22
23	24	25	26	27	28	29
30						

October

Sun	Mon	Tues	Wed	Thurs	Fri	Sat
	1	2	3	4	5	6
7	8	9	10	11	12	13
14	15	16	17	18	19	20
21	22	23	24	25	26	27
28	29	30	31			

November

Sun	Mon	Tues	Wed	Thurs	Fri	Sat
				1	2	3
4	5	6	7	8	9	10
11	12	13	14	15	16	17
18	19	20	21	22	23	24
25	26	27	28	29	30	

December

Sun	Mon	Tues	Wed	Thurs	Fri	Sat
						1
2	3	4	5	6	7	8
9	10	11	12	13	14	15
16	17	18	19	20	21	22
23	24	25	26	27	28	29
30	31					

Class Activity

Vocabulary	
month	day
week	elapsed time

▶**Use a Calendar**

Use the calendars on pages 383–384 to complete exercises 1–3.

1. What is the fourth **month** of the year?

   _____

2. What is the date of the twenty-second **day** of the third month?

   _____

3. What day of the **week** is the third day of the seventh month?

   _____

▶**Elapsed Time on a Calendar**

Write the elapsed time.

4. August 1 to November 1 is _____ months.

5. 7:00 A.M. May 2 to 7:00 A.M. May 19 is _____ days.

Write the month.

6. Eight months after March _____

7. Six months before December _____

Write the date.

8. Seven days after the third of July _____

9. Two weeks after November 2 _____

10. Four days before June 10 _____

11. One week before August 23 _____

▶ Solve Problems About Elapsed Time on a Calendar

Solve.

Show your work.

12. Garnetta worked on her project from October 4 to October 11. She then had 4 more days to complete it. How many days did she work on her project?

_____

13. David's family left for their vacation on June 3. After 2 weeks, they returned home. What date did they arrive home?

_____

14. Randi planted flower seeds in the house on January 15. On May 15, she planted the small plants outside. Three months later, they bloomed. How long did it take the seeds to grow into blooming plants?

_____

15. Irene went to the aquarium on July 16. Bruce went to the aquarium 1 week later. Chantal went to the aquarium 4 days after Bruce. On what date did Chantal go to the aquarium?

_____

16. Marilyn went to the History Museum on August 5. Alison went 1 week later. If Charlie went to the History Museum 3 days before Alison, what date did he go?

_____

▶ Elapsed Time in Minutes and Hours

17. Find the elapsed time.

Start Time	End Time	Elapsed Time
4:00 P.M.	7:00 P.M.	
7:45 A.M.	8:15 A.M.	
2:17 P.M.	7:17 P.M.	
11:00 A.M.	2:00 P.M.	
11:55 A.M.	4:25 P.M.	

18. Find the end time.

Start Time	Elapsed Time	End Time
1:00 P.M.	2 hours	
4:15 A.M.	4 hours	
4:55 P.M.	18 minutes	
2:15 A.M.	1 hour and 15 minutes	
11:55 A.M.	2 hours and 5 minutes	

19. Find the start time.

Start Time	Elapsed Time	End Time
	3 hours	4:15 P.M.
	15 minutes	2:45 P.M.
	2 hours and 35 minutes	11:55 A.M.
	1 hour and 20 minutes	3:42 A.M.

Name _____ **Date** _____

Class Activity

▶ Solve Problems About Elapsed Time on a Clock

Solve. Use your clock if you need to.

Show your work.

20. Loretta left her friend's house at 3:45. She had been there for 2 hours and 20 minutes. What time did she get there?

_____

21. Berto spent from 3:45 P.M. to 4:15 P.M. doing math homework and from 4:30 P.M. to 5:10 P.M. doing social studies homework. How much time did he spend on his math and social studies homework?

_____

22. Ed arrived at a biking trail at 9:00 A.M. He biked for 1 hour and 45 minutes. He spent 20 minutes riding home. What time did he get home?

_____

23. Mario finished swimming at 10:45. He swam for 1 hour and 15 minutes. What time did he start?

_____

24. Vasco finished cleaning his room at 4:30. It took him 25 minutes. What time did he start?

_____

25. Eric has basketball practice from 3:30 P.M. to 4:15 P.M. He has violin practice at 5:30. Today basketball practice ended 30 minutes late and it takes Eric 15 minutes to walk to violin practice. Will he be on time? Explain.

_____

_____

Elapsed Time

▶ Rotations of the Minute Hand
The clocks on this page show the movement of the minute hand.

1. The minute hand has traveled one quarter of the way around the clock.

_____ minutes have passed. The minute hand has rotated _____ degrees.

2. The minute hand has traveled halfway around the clock.

_____ minutes have passed. The minute hand has rotated _____ degrees.

3. The minute hand has traveled three quarters of the way around the clock.

_____ minutes have passed. The minute hand has rotated _____ degrees.

4. The minute hand has traveled all the way around the clock.

_____ minutes have passed. The minute hand has rotated _____ degrees.

Find how many minutes have passed and how many degrees the minute hand has rotated.

5.

minutes: _____
degrees: _____

6.

minutes: _____
degrees: _____

7.

minutes: _____
degrees: _____

8.

minutes: _____
degrees: _____

Vocabulary

degrees

▶Degrees of Rotation in 1 Minute

The minute hand rotates 6 degrees (°) in 1 minute.
Complete the sentence.

9. Between 12:00 and 12:08, the minute hand rotates _____ degrees.

10. Between 12:00 and 12:07, the minute hand rotates _____ degrees.

11. Between 12:00 and 12:10, the minute hand rotates _____ degrees.

▶Elapsed Time

Complete the sentence.

12. From 4:16 to 4:25, _____ minutes pass. The minute hand rotates

_____ degrees.

13. From 2:43 to 2:48, _____ minutes pass. The minute hand rotates

_____ degrees.

14. From 8:55 to 9:01, _____ minutes pass. The minute hand rotates

_____ degrees.

15. From 12:59 to 1:01, _____ minutes pass. The minute hand rotates

_____ degrees.

▶Find End Times Using Clock Angles

Solve.

16. A clock starts at 4:15. What time is it after the minute hand rotates

18 degrees? _____

17. A clock starts at 7:57. What time is it after the minute hand rotates

24 degrees? _____

18. A clock starts at 10:59. What time is it after the minute hand rotates

42 degrees? _____

Clock Angles

Write each time on the digital clock. Then write how to say the time.

1.

| : |

_____

2.

| : |

_____

3.

| : |

_____

4.

| : |

_____

Write the time as minutes after an hour and minutes before an hour.

5.

_____

_____

6.

_____

_____

Solve.

Show your work.

7. Diego went to his grandparents' house on August 3. He stayed there until August 21. How many days did he stay at his grandparents' house?

_____

8. At 8:45 Tamara went to basketball practice. Her practice lasted 1 hour and 15 minutes. What time did she finish her practice?

_____

9. A clock shows 7:00. What time is it after the minute hand rotates 90°? Use the clock in exercise 1 if you need to.

_____

10. **Extended Response** Carla finished her homework at 8:30. She had spent 30 minutes on math and 45 minutes on a science report. Show what time she started her homework on the clock below.

Explain how you found your answer.

_____

_____

_____

Test

Dear Family,

In this unit, your child will be introduced to fractions. Students will build fractions from unit fractions and explore fractions as parts of a whole and parts of a set.

Unit Fraction

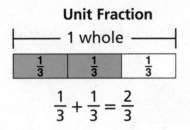

$$\frac{1}{3} + \frac{1}{3} = \frac{2}{3}$$

Fraction of a Whole

$\frac{3}{4}$ ← numerator
← denominator

Fraction of a Set

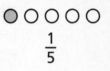

$\frac{1}{5}$

Students will find a fraction of a number.

$\frac{2}{3}$ of 12 is 8

Students will also find equivalent fractions, and compare, add, and subtract fractions.

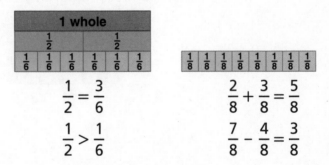

$$\frac{1}{2} = \frac{3}{6}$$

$$\frac{1}{2} > \frac{1}{6}$$

$$\frac{2}{8} + \frac{3}{8} = \frac{5}{8}$$

$$\frac{7}{8} - \frac{4}{8} = \frac{3}{8}$$

In this unit, your child will also be introduced to division with remainders.

$$8\overline{)75} \quad 9\ R3$$

Please call if you have any questions or comments.

Sincerely,
Your child's teacher

Estimada familia:

En esta unidad su niño conocerá las fracciones pro primera vez. Los estudiantes formarán fracciones a partir de fracciones cuyo numerador es uno y explorarán las fracciones como partes de un todo y partes de un conjunto.

Fracción cuyo numerador es uno

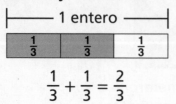

$$\frac{1}{3} + \frac{1}{3} = \frac{2}{3}$$

Fracción de un todo

$$\frac{3}{4} \leftarrow \text{numerador} \\ \phantom{\frac{3}{4}} \leftarrow \text{denominador}$$

Fracción de un conju

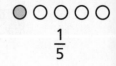

$$\frac{1}{5}$$

Los estudiantes hallarán una fracción de un número.

$\frac{2}{3}$ de 12 son 8

Los estudiantes también hallarán fracciones equivalentes y compararán, sumarán y restarán fracciones.

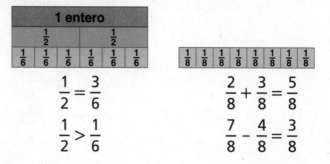

$$\frac{1}{2} = \frac{3}{6}$$

$$\frac{1}{2} > \frac{1}{6}$$

$$\frac{2}{8} + \frac{3}{8} = \frac{5}{8}$$

$$\frac{7}{8} - \frac{4}{8} = \frac{3}{8}$$

En esta unidad su niño también conocerá por primera vez la división con residuos.

$$8\overline{)75} \quad 9\ R3$$

Si tiene alguna duda o comentario, por favor comuníquese conmigo.

Atentamente,
El maestro de su niño

Class Activity

►Use a Bar Graph to Compare

Use the bar graph below to complete exercises 1–4.

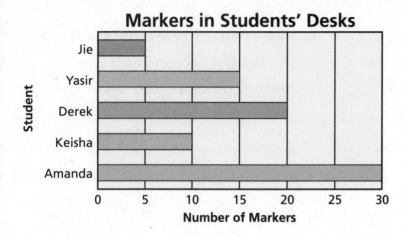

Markers in Students' Desks

Fill in the blanks.

1. Jie has _____ as many markers as Yasir has.

   Yasir has _____ as many markers as Jie has.

2. Derek has _____ as many markers as Jie has.

   Jie has _____ as many markers as Derek has.

3. Derek has _____ as many markers as Keisha has.

   Keisha has _____ as many markers as Derek has.

4. Amanda has _____ as many markers as Yasir has.

   Yasir has _____ as many markers as Amanda has.

▶ Solve Comparison Word Problems

Solve each problem. Then write the other comparing sentence. The first one is done for you.

5. Carmen rides the train 7 miles to work. Joe rides 6 times as far as Carmen. How far does Joe ride the train? _____42 miles_____

Carmen rides $\frac{1}{6}$ as far as Joe. _____

_____

6. Ben read 28 books last summer. His brother Ryan read $\frac{1}{7}$ as many books as Ben. How many books did Ryan read? _____

_____

_____

7. Kurt has 8 CDs. Julie has 4 times as many CDs as Kurt. How many CDs does Julie have? _____

_____

_____

8. A cheetah can run 70 miles per hour. A rabbit runs about $\frac{1}{2}$ as fast as a cheetah. How fast can a rabbit run? _____

_____

_____

9. The Knights won 36 basketball games last season. The Spartans won $\frac{1}{9}$ as many games. How many games did the Spartans win? _____

_____

_____

10. Raul's father weighs 180 pounds. Raul weighs $\frac{1}{3}$ as much as his father. How much does Raul weigh? _____

_____

_____

11. Lon has 9 books. Jerome has 6 times as many books as Lon has. How many books does Jerome have? _____

_____

_____

12. Barry's father is 48 years old. Barry is $\frac{1}{6}$ as old as his father. How old is Barry? _____

_____

_____

Name _____ **Date** _____

Class Activity

▶ More Comparison Statements

Use the bar graph below for Exercises 1–5.

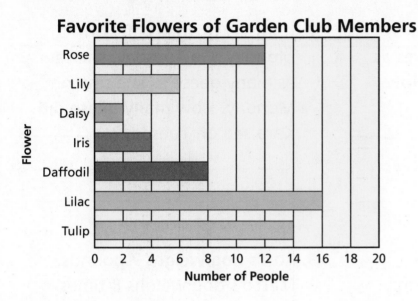

Favorite Flowers of Garden Club Members

Fill in the blanks.

1. _____ as many people like daffodils as like daisies.

   _____ as many people like daisies as like daffodils.

2. _____ as many people like lilacs as like daffodils.

   _____ as many people like daffodils as like lilacs.

3. _____ as many people like irises as like lilacs.

   _____ as many people like lilacs as like irises.

4. _____ as many people like lilies as like roses.

   _____ as many people like roses as like lilies.

5. **Write Your Own** Write two comparison statements involving the number of people who like daisies.

_____

_____

Name _____   **Date** _____

Class Activity

►More Comparison Word Problems

Solve each problem. Then write the other comparing sentence.

6. Reyna caught 6 fish. Her grandfather caught 4 times as many fish as Reyna did. How many fish did Reyna's grandfather catch? _____

_____

_____

7. Kara saw 42 geese fly on Monday. On Tuesday, she saw $\frac{1}{7}$ as many geese as she saw on Monday. How many geese did Kara see on Tuesday? _____

_____

_____

8. There are 72 chairs in the lunchroom. In the basement, there are $\frac{1}{9}$ as many chairs as there are in the lunchroom. How many chairs are in the basement? _____

_____

_____

9. Rosi's dog weighs 7 pounds. Marco's dog weighs 8 times as much as Rosi's dog. What is the weight of Marco's dog? _____

_____

_____

10. Scott and his grandmother made a quilt. Scott's grandmother sewed 36 of the quilt squares. Scott sewed $\frac{1}{6}$ as many quilt squares as his grandmother. How many quilt squares did Scott sew? _____

_____

_____

11. Juanita delivered 35 newspapers. Her younger brother delivered $\frac{1}{7}$ as many newspapers as Juanita did. How many newspapers did her brother deliver? _____

_____

_____

Practice Fractional Comparisons

▶ Explore Fractional Parts of a Set

1. The Promo Company prints T-shirts for the rock band
   MathGrlzz. Complete the table to show how many
   shirts of each size and color they printed on Monday.

MathGrlzz Shirts Printed on Monday

	$\frac{1}{6}$ Yellow	$\frac{2}{6}$ Red	$\frac{3}{6}$ Blue
18 small shirts			
36 medium shirts			
54 large shirts			
48 extra large shirts			

2. The Promo Company also prints caps and hats for
   MathGrlzz. Complete the table to show how many caps
   or hats of each type and color they printed on Monday.

MathGrlzz Caps and Hats Printed on Monday

	$\frac{1}{7}$ Yellow	$\frac{4}{7}$ Red	$\frac{2}{7}$ Blue
49 baseball caps			
21 knit caps			
35 floppy hats			
14 straw hats			

Name _____ **Date** _____

Class Activity

►Solve Problems Involving a Fraction of a Set

Harry made 27 birds out of clay. He painted $\frac{4}{9}$ of the birds blue and the rest white.

3. How many birds did he paint blue? _____

4. How many birds did he paint white? _____

5. What fraction of the birds did he paint white?

_____

6. Tameka wrote 24 word problems. Three eighths of the problems were subtraction problems. How many subtraction problems did Tameka write?

_____

7. Marcel had 15 carrot sticks in his lunch. He gave $\frac{2}{5}$ of the carrot sticks to Joni. How many carrot sticks did Marcel give to Joni?

_____

8. Karen baked 48 muffins. She gave $\frac{5}{8}$ of the muffins to her cousin. How many muffins did Karen give to her cousin?

_____

9. There are 36 trees in a section of woods. Four ninths of the trees are oak trees. How many oak trees are there?

_____

Show your work.

Find a Fraction of a Set or a Number

Name _____   Date _____

▶ Write a Rule

10. Write a rule for finding a fraction of a set or a number.

_____

_____

_____

_____

_____

_____

▶ Use a Rule

Use your rule to find each amount.

11. $\frac{2}{4}$ of 12 _____

12. $\frac{2}{6}$ of 30 _____

13. $\frac{5}{7}$ of 35 _____

14. $\frac{2}{2} \times 16$ _____

15. $\frac{4}{6} \times 36$ _____

16. $\frac{5}{9}$ of 81 _____

17. $\frac{7}{8} \times 56$ _____

18. $\frac{2}{3} \times 30$ _____

19. $\frac{5}{6}$ of 18 _____

20. $\frac{3}{8}$ of 32 _____

21. $\frac{7}{10} \times 40$ _____

22. $\frac{3}{4}$ of 24 _____

Going Further

▶ Solve a Problem by Acting It Out

1. Olivia picked 28 daisies. She gave $\frac{5}{7}$ of the daisies to her aunt. Olivia kept the rest of the daisies. How many daisies did Olivia keep?

_____

2. Cesar bought 16 baseball cards. He kept $\frac{5}{8}$ of the cards. He gave the rest of the cards to his friend. How many cards did Cesar give to his friend?

_____

3. Pavel's father bought a box of 18 pencils. He gave $\frac{2}{9}$ of the pencils to Pavel and $\frac{2}{9}$ of the pencils to Pavel's sister Helena. How many pencils were left?

_____

4. Akio had 21 stickers. He gave $\frac{3}{7}$ of the stickers to Rich and $\frac{1}{7}$ of the stickers to Imani. Akio kept the rest of the stickers. How many stickers did Akio keep?

_____

5. Gianna had 25 postcards. She gave $\frac{1}{5}$ of the postcards to her sister. She gave $\frac{1}{4}$ of the remaining postcards to her brother. Gianna kept the rest of the postcards. How many postcards did she keep?

_____

6. Mr. Redbird caught 32 fish. He gave $\frac{1}{4}$ of the fish to his brother. He kept $\frac{3}{4}$ of the remaining fish for his family. He gave the rest of the fish to his neighbor. How many fish did Mr. Redbird give to his neighbor?

_____

Class Activity

Name _____ Date _____

Vocabulary

circle graph

▶ Read a Circle Graph

Kari has 36 animals in her beanbag collection. This **circle graph** shows the fraction of the whole collection for each type of animal. For example, $\frac{1}{6}$ of the animals in her collection are rabbits.

Kari's Beanbag Animal Collection

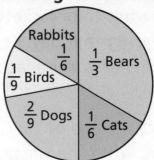

1. Complete the table.

Type of Animal	Fraction of Whole Collection	Number of Animals
Birds		
Rabbits		
Bears		
Cats		
Dogs		

Complete.

2. What type of beanbag animal does Kari have the most of?

_____

3. What type of beanbag animal does Kari have the least of?

_____

4. What fraction of the collection are the birds and dogs combined?

_____

5. What fraction of the collection are the bears and cats combined?

_____

Class Activity

▶Label and Use a Circle Graph

Ms. Timmer's class made a graph
to show what color jackets students
were wearing that day. There are
24 students who wore jackets.

**Jacket Colors in
Ms. Timmer's Class**

6. In each section of the circle
   graph, write the fraction
   for the color.

7. Complete the table.

Jacket Color	Fraction of All Students	Number of Students
Pink		
Blue		
Yellow		
Green		

Complete.

8. Which color jacket did most of
   the students wear?

   _____

9. What fraction of the class wore
   yellow or blue jackets?

   _____

10. How many more students wore
    green jackets than yellow
    jackets?

    _____

11. What fraction of the class wore
    blue, yellow, or green jackets?

    _____

Fractions on Circle Graphs

Class Activity

▶ **Use the Language of Probability**

Probability describes how likely it is that something will happen. You can use words or a number from 0 to 1 to describe it.

Vocabulary

probability
likely
unlikely
certain
impossible
equally likely
event

Use the spinner at the right. Write the words *likely, unlikely, equally likely, impossible,* or *certain* to describe the likelihood of the event.

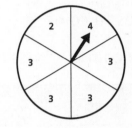

1. Spinning a 2 _____

2. Spinning a 3 _____

3. Spinning either a 2 or a 4 _____

4. Spinning a 5 _____

5. Spinning a number less than 5 _____

▶ **Record Probability in Two Ways**

Use the spinner above to write the probability of the event.

6. What is the probability of spinning a 3?

   _____ out of _____ or ☐/☐

7. What is the probability of spinning a 2?

   _____ out of _____ or ☐/☐

8. What is the probability of spinning a 4?

   _____ out of _____ or ☐/☐

9. What is the probability of spinning a 1?

   _____

10. What is the probability of spinning a number less than 5?

   _____

Name _____ **Date** _____

Class Activity

▶ Conduct a Coin Toss Experiment

When you toss a coin, heads or tails are equally likely to land up. This means they have the same chance of occurring. Heads has a 1 out of 2 chance of happening. You can expect to get heads about half the time, or about 1 out of every 2 tosses.

11. What is the probability written as a fraction of heads landing up when

    you toss a coin? _____

12. Toss a coin 20 times and keep a tally.

Heads	Tails

13. How many tosses did you make? _____

14. I tossed heads _____ out of _____ tosses.

15. I tossed tails _____ out of _____ tosses.

16. Did you get heads for about $\frac{1}{2}$ of your tosses? _____

17. **Explain** If the probability of getting heads is $\frac{1}{2}$, why do you think you and your partner may not have tossed heads half of the time?

    _____

    _____

18. Work with your teacher to combine the results for your class.

    Class results: Heads: _____ Tails: _____

    Did your class get heads closer to one half than you did in exercise 14?

    _____

Explore Probability

Class Activity

Name _____

Date _____

▶ Make and Test Predictions

Use the rectangles at the right to make predictions about a probability experiment.

19. Suppose you cut out the 10 rectangles, place them in a bag and pull a rectangle out of the bag without looking. Write the probability of pulling each color rectangle.

    Blue Rectangle _____ out of _____ or _____

    Yellow Rectangle _____ out of _____ or _____

20. Suppose you pull a rectangle out of the bag without looking 20 times. After each pull, you return the rectangle back into the bag. Predict which color rectangle you think you will pull out more times. Explain.

    _____

    _____

    _____

21. Cut out the 10 rectangles on page 416A or Activity Workbook page 189 and place them in a bag. Conduct the experiment described in exercise 20. Record the results in a tally chart.

22. Was your prediction correct? _____

23. If you conducted the experiment again, predict if the results will be exactly the same.

    _____

    _____

    _____

    _____

Class Activity

▶ What's in the Bag?

Use the paper bag with the 10 coins (dimes and pennies) that another Student Pair prepared for you to conduct this experiment. Predict how many of each type of coin is in the bag.

Here's what to do:

Step 1: Without looking into the bag, pull a coin out and record the type of coin in the tally chart below.

Dimes	Pennies
Total:	Total:

Step 2: Return the coin to the bag.

Step 3: Take turns doing this until each of you has done this 20 times.

Step 4: Use the results to make a prediction of how many dimes and how many pennies are in your bag.

Dimes _____ Pennies _____

Step 5: Look into the bag and check your prediction.

Explain how you made your prediction.

_____

_____

_____

_____

Explore Probability

▶Probability Experiments

Carefully cut out each rectangle along the dashed lines. Use the cut outs for probability experiments on Student Book pages 415 and 418.

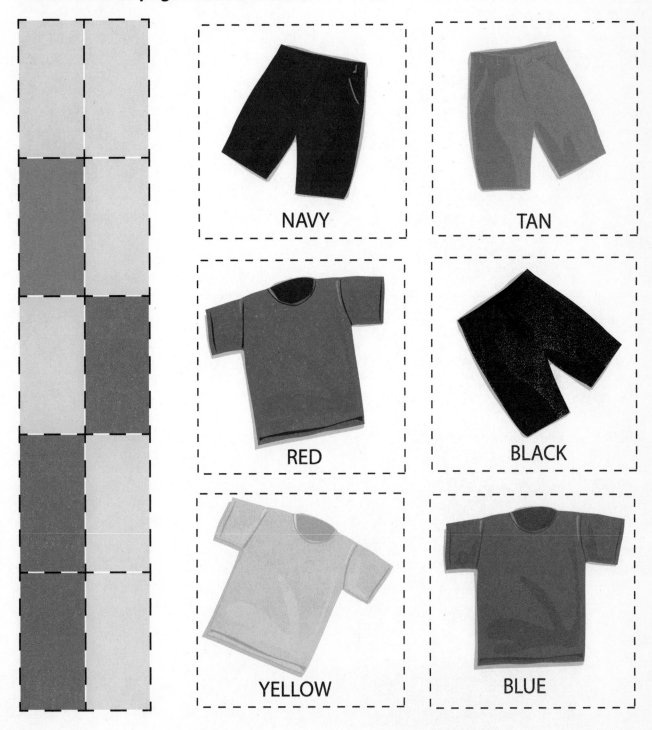

NAVY

TAN

RED

BLACK

YELLOW

BLUE

Discover Probability

Class Activity

Vocabulary

outcome

▶List Outcomes

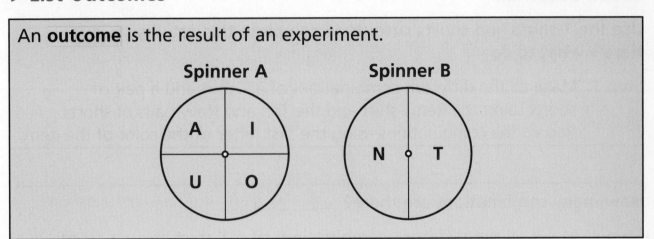

An **outcome** is the result of an experiment.

Spinner A   **Spinner B**

A I U O   N T

Complete.

1. Look at both spinners. Make an organized list of all the possible pairs of letters you could get if you spin Spinner A and then Spinner B.

2. How many pairs can you make? _____

3. Cross off any pairs that don't make a two-letter word.

   How many two-letter words can you make? _____

4. Is the probability of spinning a word more or less than half?

_____

▶Conduct a Spinner Experiment

5. Make the spinners from Spin a Word (TRB M161). Spin both spinners 10 times and record the pairs you spin.

6. How many words did you spin? _____

7. Was this more or less than half of your spins? _____

Name _____   **Date** _____

Class Activity

▶ Combinations

Use the T-shirts and shorts cutouts to complete this activity.
Here's what to do:

Step 1: Make all the different combinations of a T-shirt and a pair of shorts using the Red T-shirt and the Tan and Navy pairs of shorts. Record the combinations using the first letter of the color of the item.

How many combinations are there? _____

Step 2: Make all the different combinations of a T-shirt and a pair of shorts using the Red and Yellow T-shirts and the Tan and Navy pairs of shorts. Record the combinations using the first letter of the color of the item.

How many combinations are there? _____

Step 3: Make all the different combinations of a T-shirt and a pair of shorts using the three T-shirts and the Tan and Navy pairs of shorts. Record the combinations using the first letter of the color of the item.

How many combinations are there? _____

Step 4: Make all the different combinations of a T-Shirt and a pair of shorts using the three T-shirts and all three pairs of shorts. Record the combinations using the first letter of the color of the item.

How many combinations are there? _____

What pattern do you see?

_____

_____

Explore Probability

▶Play *Spinning a Whole*

Play *Spinning a Whole* with your partner. Write down anything interesting you discover while playing the game.

Rules for *Spinning a Whole*

Number of players: 2 or 3
What You Will Need: a Gameboard for Halves or Thirds and matching pair of spinners for each player, paper clip, ruler

1. On each turn, a player chooses and spins one of the two spinners.

2. Using the labeled fraction bars as a guide, the player marks and shades a section of the whole to represent the fraction the spinner landed on.

   • On a player's first turn, the player starts at the left end of the whole.

   • On other turns, the player starts at the right end of the last section shaded.

3. If a player spins a fraction greater than the unshaded portion of the whole, the player does not shade anything on his or her turn.

4. The first player to fill his or her whole bar completely and exactly wins.

Play *Spinning a Whole*

Game Board for Halves

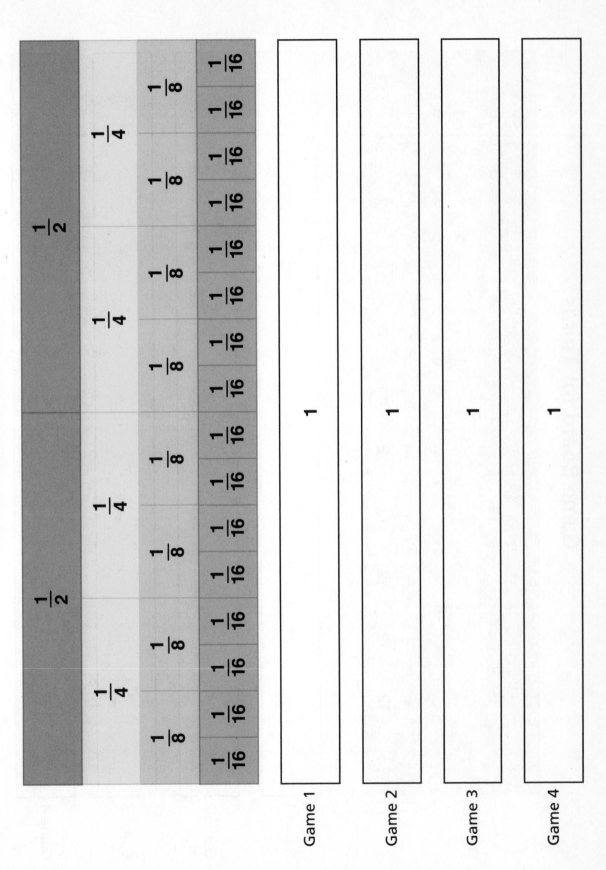

Game Board for Thirds

$\frac{1}{3}$	$\frac{1}{6}$	$\frac{1}{12}$
		$\frac{1}{12}$
	$\frac{1}{6}$	$\frac{1}{12}$
		$\frac{1}{12}$
$\frac{1}{3}$	$\frac{1}{6}$	$\frac{1}{12}$
		$\frac{1}{12}$
	$\frac{1}{6}$	$\frac{1}{12}$
		$\frac{1}{12}$
$\frac{1}{3}$	$\frac{1}{6}$	$\frac{1}{12}$
		$\frac{1}{12}$
	$\frac{1}{6}$	$\frac{1}{12}$
		$\frac{1}{12}$

Game 1 — 1

Game 2 — 1

Game 3 — 1

Game 4 — 1

Game Board for Thirds

Spinners for Halves

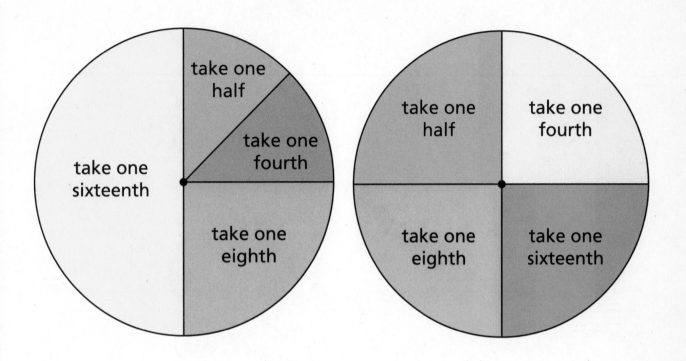

Spinners for Thirds

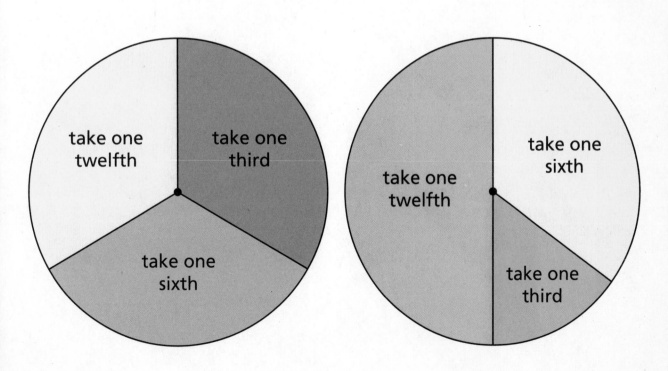

Spinners for Halves and Thirds

Multiplication Table Rows

1	2	3	4	5	6	7	8	9	10
1	2	3	4	5	6	7	8	9	10
2	4	6	8	10	12	14	16	18	20
3	6	9	12	15	18	21	24	27	30
4	8	12	16	20	24	28	32	36	40
5	10	15	20	25	30	35	40	45	50
6	12	18	24	30	36	42	48	54	60
7	14	21	28	35	42	49	56	63	70
8	16	24	32	40	48	56	64	72	80
9	18	27	36	45	54	63	72	81	90
10	20	30	40	50	60	70	80	90	100

Equivalent Fraction Box

×1	×2	×3	×4	×5	×6	×7	×8	×9	×10

	=	=	=	=	=	=	=	=	=

×1	×2	×3	×4	×5	×6	×7	×8	×9	×10

Class Activity

Add. Use the fraction strips to help you.

9. $\frac{3}{7} + \frac{2}{7} =$ _____

10. $\frac{3}{9} + \frac{5}{9} =$ _____

11. $\frac{6}{11} + \frac{2}{11} =$ _____

12. $\frac{4}{12} + \frac{7}{12} =$ _____

13. $\frac{2}{3} + \frac{2}{9} =$ _____

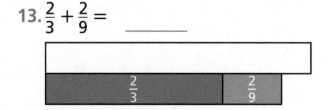

14. $\frac{5}{8} + \frac{3}{16} =$ _____

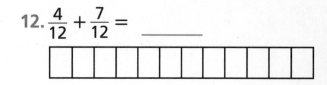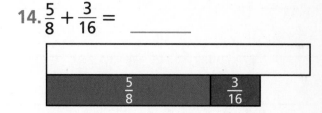

15. $\frac{3}{4} + \frac{3}{12} =$ _____

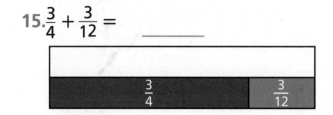

16. $\frac{2}{3} + \frac{1}{5} =$ _____

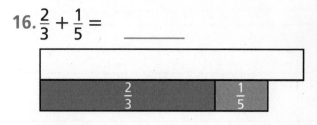

17. $\frac{1}{4} + \frac{1}{6} =$ _____

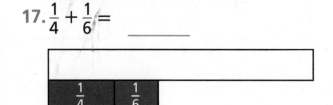

18. $\frac{3}{6} + \frac{1}{4} =$ _____

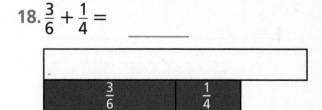

19. $\frac{1}{2} + \frac{2}{5} =$ _____

20. $\frac{1}{3} + \frac{2}{4} =$ _____

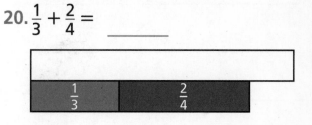

21. **On the Back** Explain how you found the answer to exercise 18.

_____

_____

_____

_____

_____

_____

_____

_____

_____

_____

_____

_____

_____

▶ **Add, Compare, and Subtract Fractions**

Add, compare, and subtract each pair of fractions.

Add	Compare	Subtract
30. $\frac{3}{8} + \frac{5}{8} =$ _____	$\frac{3}{8} \bigcirc \frac{5}{8}$	
31. $\frac{1}{4} + \frac{1}{3} =$ _____	$\frac{1}{4} \bigcirc \frac{1}{3}$	
32. $\frac{1}{3} + \frac{1}{2} =$ _____	$\frac{1}{3} \bigcirc \frac{1}{2}$	
33. $\frac{5}{6} + \frac{1}{3}$ _____	$\frac{5}{6} \bigcirc \frac{1}{3}$	
34. $\frac{1}{2} + \frac{2}{4} =$ _____	$\frac{1}{2} \bigcirc \frac{2}{4}$	

Class Activity

▶ Fractions in Word Problems

Solve.

Show your work.

35. Layton ate $\frac{1}{6}$ of the cake. Kyra ate $\frac{3}{6}$ of the cake. Who ate more cake? How much more?

_____

36. Jorie ate $\frac{5}{6}$ of her popsicle. Nat ate $\frac{3}{4}$ of his popsicle. Who ate more? How much more?

_____

37. One fourth of the cars in the parking lot are red. Three eighths of the cars are blue. Are there more red cars or more blue cars?

_____

38. The red squirrel ate $\frac{2}{3}$ of the acorns. The gray squirrel ate $\frac{1}{4}$ of the acorns. What fraction of the acorns did they eat altogether?

_____

39. Camille has two cats, Cole and Nicky. Every day, Cole eats $\frac{1}{3}$ of a can of food. Nicky eats $\frac{4}{6}$ of a can of food. How much of the can do the two cats eat together?

_____

40. Oakton School and Pine School use the same amount of paper. Oakton recycles $\frac{3}{4}$ of its paper. Pine recycles $\frac{2}{4}$ of its paper. How much more of its paper does Oakton recycle than Pine recycles?

_____

Compare and Subtract Fractions

Class Activity

▶Identify and Locate Whole Numbers on a Number Line

You can use points already on a number line to locate and label other points. Locate the points for the numbers 150 and 375 on the number line and label them.

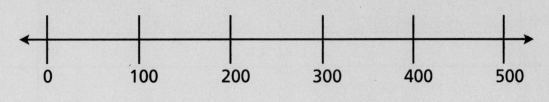

Locate the points for the numbers and label them.

1. 35, 18, 45, 90, 75

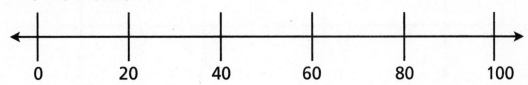

2. 90, 225, 425, 275, 380

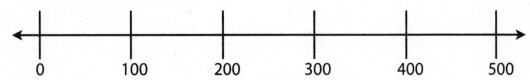

▶Find the Distance Between Two Points

Locate the points for the numbers on the number line and label them. Then use the number line to find the distance between the two points.

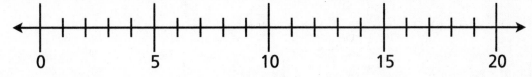

3. 17 and 8 _____   **4.** 15 and 7 _____   **5.** 12 and 8 _____

6. 11 and 4 _____   **7.** 14 and 9 _____   **8.** 20 and 10 _____

Name _____   Date _____

▶Identify and Locate Fractions on a Number Line

The number lines and fraction bars below show the halves and fourths between 0 and 1.

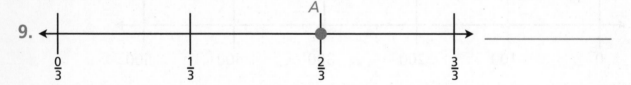

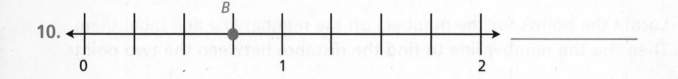

Write the fraction or whole number and fraction for each lettered point.

9.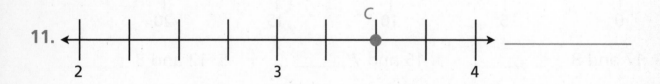

10.

11.

Class Activity

▶ Fraction, Decimals, and Money

Equal shares of 1 whole can be written as a fraction or as a decimal. Each whole dollar below is equal to 100 pennies. Discuss the patterns you see.

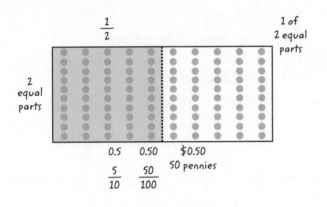

$\frac{1}{2}$ 1 of 2 equal parts

2 equal parts

0.5   0.50 $0.50
$\frac{5}{10}$ $\frac{50}{100}$ 50 pennies

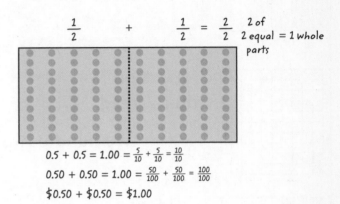

$\frac{1}{2}$ + $\frac{1}{2}$ = $\frac{2}{2}$ 2 of 2 equal = 1 whole parts

$0.5 + 0.5 = 1.00 = \frac{5}{10} + \frac{5}{10} = \frac{10}{10}$

$0.50 + 0.50 = 1.00 = \frac{50}{100} + \frac{50}{100} = \frac{100}{100}$

$\$0.50 + \$0.50 = \$1.00$

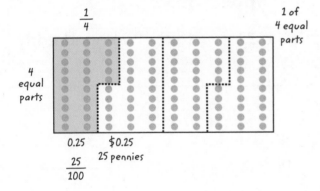

$\frac{1}{4}$ 1 of 4 equal parts

4 equal parts

0.25 $0.25
$\frac{25}{100}$ 25 pennies

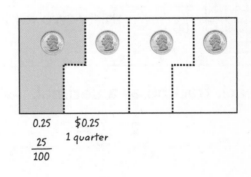

$\frac{1}{4}$ 1 of 4 equal parts

4 equal parts

0.25 $0.25
$\frac{25}{100}$ 1 quarter

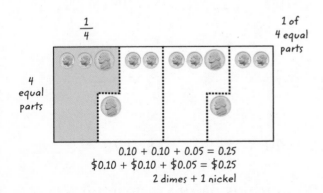

$\frac{1}{4}$ 1 of 4 equal parts

4 equal parts

$0.10 + 0.10 + 0.05 = 0.25$
$\$0.10 + \$0.10 + \$0.05 = \$0.25$
2 dimes + 1 nickel

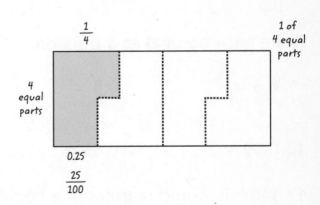

$\frac{1}{4}$ 1 of 4 equal parts

4 equal parts

0.25
$\frac{25}{100}$

Class Activity

Name _____ **Date** _____

Vocabulary

decimal
decimal point
tenths
hundredths

►Tenths and Hundredths

Fractions can be written as **decimals**.

	Fraction	Decimal
	write: read:	write: read:
	$\frac{3}{10}$ three **tenths**	0.3 three tenths

↑
└─ **decimal point**

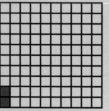

	Fraction	Decimal
	write: read:	write: read:
	$\frac{2}{100}$ two **hundredths**	0.02 two hundredths

	Fraction	Decimal
	write: read:	write: read:
	$\frac{32}{100}$ thirty-two hundredths	0.32 thirty-two hundredths

Write each fraction as a decimal.

1. $\frac{1}{10}$ = _____   2. $\frac{5}{10}$ = _____   3. $\frac{9}{10}$ = _____   4. $\frac{6}{10}$ = _____

5. $\frac{34}{100}$ = _____   6. $\frac{50}{100}$ = _____   7. $\frac{6}{100}$ = _____   8. $\frac{85}{100}$ = _____

Write each decimal as a fraction.

9. 0.8 = _____   10. 0.5 = _____   11. 0.7 = _____   12. 0.2 = _____

13. 0.09 = _____   14. 0.65 = _____   15. 0.40 = _____   16. 0.72 = _____

17. Jeb has 72 red marbles in a bag of 100 marbles. Write a decimal that represents the red marbles as a part of all the marbles in the bag.

_____

Fractions and Decimals

Class Activity

▶ Decimals Greater than 1

These models show decimals greater than 1.

Write: **Read:**

2.3   two and three tenths

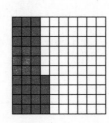

2.34   two and thirty-four hundredths

Write a decimal for the shaded part.

18.

_____

19.

_____

20.

_____

21.

_____

▶ Equivalent Decimals

Write an equivalent decimal.

22. 0.4 = _____   23. 0.90 = _____   24. 0.60 = _____   25. 0.7 = _____

26. 0.50 = _____   27. 0.20 = _____   28. 2.8 = _____   29. 1.90 = _____

Class Activity

▶ Compare and Order Decimals

Write >, < or = in the ◯ .

30. $0.25 ◯ $0.35

31. 0.5 ◯ 0.15

32. $0.50 ◯ $0.45

_____

33. 0.6 ◯ 0.60

34. $0.77 ◯ $0.88

35. 0.85 ◯ 0.7

_____

36. $0.95 ◯ $1.00

37. $1.77 ◯ $2.88

38. 2.7 ◯ 1.75

_____

Write these amounts in order from least to greatest.

39. $\frac{1}{2}$ dollar, $0.45, $0.75

40. $\frac{1}{4}$ of a dollar, $0.55, $0.15

_____ _____

41. 0.7, 0.42, 0.84

_____

▶ Compare Fractions and Decimals on a Number Line

Circle the lengths to show each fraction and decimal.
Then compare. Write <, >, or = in the ◯ .

42. $\frac{1}{2}$ ◯ 0.6

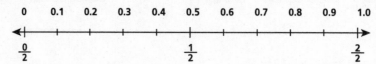

43. $\frac{1}{4}$ ◯ 0.3

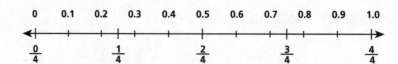

44. $\frac{3}{4}$ ◯ 0.7

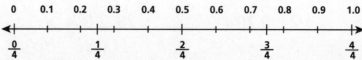

Fractions and Decimals

Class Activity

▶ Use Models to Visualize Mixed Numbers and Improper Fractions

Write the mixed number and improper fraction that the drawing shows.

1.

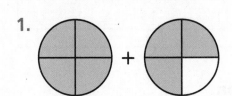

$1 + \dfrac{3}{4} = 1\dfrac{3}{4}$

$\dfrac{4}{4} + \dfrac{3}{4} = \dfrac{7}{4}$

2.

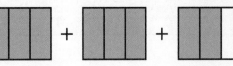

$1 + \underline{} + \underline{} = \underline{}$

$\dfrac{3}{3} + \underline{} + \underline{} = \underline{}$

3.

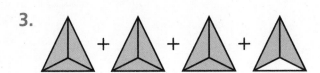

$1 + \underline{} + \underline{} + \underline{} = \underline{}$

$\dfrac{3}{3} + \underline{} + \underline{} + \underline{} = \underline{}$

4.

$1 + \underline{} = \underline{}$

$\underline{} + \underline{} = \underline{}$

5.

$1 + \underline{} = \underline{}$

$\underline{} + \underline{} = \underline{}$

6.

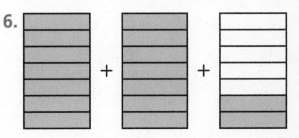

$1 + \underline{} + \underline{} = \underline{}$

$\dfrac{7}{7} + \underline{} + \underline{} = \underline{}$

Class Activity

▶ Mixed Numbers and Improper Fractions on a Number Line

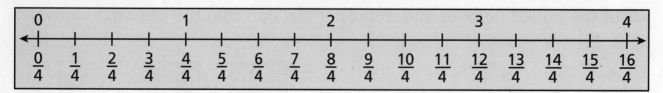

Use the number line to write the improper fraction, mixed number, or whole number.

7. $\frac{13}{4} =$ _____

8. $\frac{7}{4} =$ _____

9. $\frac{10}{4} =$ _____

10. $\frac{16}{4} =$ _____

11. $1\frac{1}{4} =$ _____

12. $2\frac{1}{4} =$ _____

13. $3\frac{1}{4} =$ _____

14. $2\frac{3}{4} =$ _____

▶ Practice with Mixed Numbers and Improper Fractions

Write the improper fraction or mixed number.

15. $2\frac{3}{5} =$ _____

16. $\frac{8}{6} =$ _____

17. $1\frac{2}{7} =$ _____

18. $\frac{11}{9} =$ _____

$\frac{5}{5} + \frac{5}{5} + \frac{3}{5} = \frac{13}{5}$

19. $1\frac{5}{8} =$ _____

20. $3\frac{1}{2} =$ _____

21. $\frac{19}{4} =$ _____

22. $\frac{7}{5} =$ _____

23. $\frac{10}{3} =$ _____

24. $2\frac{1}{6} =$ _____

25. $1\frac{3}{9} =$ _____

26. $\frac{11}{7} =$ _____

Improper Fractions and Mixed Numbers

▶ Explore Division with Remainders

Solve.

1. Hassan is making party decorations for the classroom. He needs 5 inches of string for each one. He has 15 inches of string. How many decorations can Hassan make?

2. Ana is also making decorations. She needs 5 inches of string per decoration. She has 16 inches of string. How many decorations can she make? How many inches of string will be left over?

3. Glenna is making copies of a story she wrote. She needs 4 pieces of paper per copy. She has 34 pieces of paper. How many copies can Glenna make?

4. Owen needs to pack 44 snacks into boxes. He can fit 8 snacks in each box. How many boxes does Owen need to pack all of the snacks?

5. Ty plans to write 60 math problems. He can fit 8 problems on a page. How many pages will Ty need for all 60 math problems?

6. The Science Club is renting vans for 37 people to take a field trip. Each van holds 8 people. How many vans are needed?

7. A truck company will carry 65 tons of gravel today. Each truck can hold 9 tons. How many trucks will be needed to carry the gravel?

8. Hector needs to put 9 flowers in each vase. He has 59 flowers in all. How many vases can Hector fill? How many flowers will be left over?

►Practice Dividing with Remainders

Write the answer.

9. $3\overline{)17}$ 10. $6\overline{)26}$ 11. $8\overline{)27}$ 12. $7\overline{)39}$

13. $6\overline{)40}$ 14. $9\overline{)56}$ 15. $5\overline{)48}$ 16. $2\overline{)15}$

17. $5\overline{)33}$ 18. $8\overline{)45}$ 19. $7\overline{)44}$ 20. $3\overline{)29}$

21. $4\overline{)30}$ 22. $9\overline{)71}$ 23. $3\overline{)31}$ 24. $8\overline{)63}$

25. $2\overline{)17}$ 26. $4\overline{)27}$ 27. $5\overline{)37}$ 28. $6\overline{)56}$

29. $7\overline{)54}$ 30. $8\overline{)54}$ 31. $9\overline{)73}$ 32. $10\overline{)55}$

Name _____ Date _____

►Express the Remainder as a Fraction

Write the answer with a remainder and then as a mixed number.

1. $6\overline{)56}$ 2. $8\overline{)49}$ 3. $3\overline{)17}$ 4. $7\overline{)68}$

5. $9\overline{)42}$ 6. $5\overline{)48}$ 7. $8\overline{)30}$ 8. $7\overline{)18}$

9. $4\overline{)22}$ 10. $7\overline{)36}$ 11. $6\overline{)28}$ 12. $9\overline{)88}$

13. $8\overline{)75}$ 14. $5\overline{)49}$ 15. $9\overline{)38}$ 16. $7\overline{)58}$

17. $2\overline{)19}$ 18. $3\overline{)26}$ 19. $6\overline{)53}$ 20. $8\overline{)54}$

▶Interpret Remainders

Solve.

21. At the end of each day, the 3 bakers at Ben's Bakery each take home an equal amount of leftover cake. On Tuesday, 7 cakes were left over. How much cake will each baker take home?

_____

22. A delivery man has 78 jugs of water in his truck. He will leave 9 jugs of water at each delivery stop. How many stops will he make? How many jugs will be left in his truck?

_____

23. Today 6 people went on a picnic in the park. They agreed to share 14 cups of lemonade equally. How much lemonade will each person get to drink?

_____

24. Ben's Bakery has 54 cupcakes. The bakery packs cupcakes in boxes of 8 each. How many boxes will be filled? How many cupcakes will be left over?

_____

25. Mr. Calvert has 7 cats. Each week, he divides 38 cans of cat food equally among his cats. How many cans of cat food does each cat eat per week?

_____

26. There are 89 goldfish in the fishpond. They will be put in fish tanks for the winter. If each fish tank holds 9 fish, how many tanks are needed?

_____

27. Thirty-nine people are traveling to the basketball game. If each van holds 9 people, how many vans will be needed?

_____

28. Jamal has 41 CDs. Each shelf in his CD rack holds 6 CDs. How many shelves does he need to hold all his CDs?

_____

▶ More Division Word Problems with Remainders

Solve.

1. Eileen is putting popcorn balls into bags for a party. She has 51 popcorn balls. Each bag holds 6. How many bags can Eileen fill completely? How many popcorn balls will be left over?

2. Luis is making hot chocolate for 8 friends. The friends would like to share it equally. If Luis makes 25 cups of hot chocolate, how much hot chocolate can each friend have?

3. Rey is filling the fish tanks at the zoo. He has 63 gallons of water. Each tank holds 10 gallons. How many tanks can Rey fill? How much water will be left over?

4. Lisa is putting cans on shelves in the grocery store. There are 37 cans. Each shelf holds 8 cans. How many shelves can Lisa fill? How many cans will be left over?

5. Mrs. Lin ordered 34 mini-pizzas for her niece's party. Nine girls are coming to the party. How many mini-pizzas can each girl have if the pizzas are shared equally?

6. Crystal needs to pack 40 pieces of clothing into her dresser drawers. If each drawer holds 7 pieces of clothing, how many dresser drawers does she need to fit all her clothing?

7. Sunny has 43 rings. She can put 8 rings in a jewelry box. How many jewelry boxes does Sunny need to store all the rings?

8. Emilio is arranging daisies in vases. He has 54 daisies. Each vase will hold 7 daisies. How many vases can Emilio fill?

▶ Practice Dividing with Remainders

Write the answer with a remainder and as a mixed number.

9. $23 \div 7$ _____

10. $31 \div 6$ _____

11. $75 \div 9$ _____

12. $63 \div 8$ _____

13. $44 \div 9$ _____

14. $52 \div 7$ _____

15. $85 \div 9$ _____

16. $17 \div 5$ _____

17. $38 \div 7$ _____

18. $46 \div 6$ _____

19. $67 \div 8$ _____

20. $57 \div 7$ _____

21. $43 \div 5$ _____

22. $37 \div 4$ _____

23. $79 \div 8$ _____

► Math and Art

The Ndebele people in Africa paint their houses with geometric figures.

On a separate piece of paper, draw a picture of a house. Color the house with geometric figures.

1. What figures did you use?

_____

2. How many of each figure did you use?

_____

3. Did you use parallel or perpendicular lines?

_____

4. What kind of angles did you use?

_____

5. Are any of the shapes in your design congruent?

_____

6. Is your design symmetrical?

_____

Name _____ **Date** _____

Class Activity

►The Great Game Company

The Great Game Company has asked you to help them with the spinners they make for games.

7. The company wants a fair spinner where it will be equally likely to get red, blue, or green. Which of the spinners below are fair? Which are unfair? Explain.

Spinner A   Spinner B   Spinner C

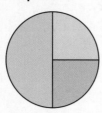   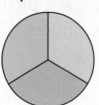   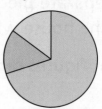

_____

_____

_____

8. The company wants a spinner where it is impossible to get blue and where it is more likely for a player to get red than green. Design a spinner for them.

Use Mathematical Processes

Name _____

Date _____

Unit Test

1. Write a fraction to represent the part of the whole that is shaded.

_____

2. What fraction of the circles are shaded?

_____

Use mental math to find the answer.

3. $\frac{1}{5} \times 40 =$ _____

4. $\frac{3}{4}$ of 24 = _____

Use the fraction strips to show the fractions are equivalent. Then fill the missing numbers in the boxes.

5. $\frac{4}{5}$ and $\frac{8}{10}$

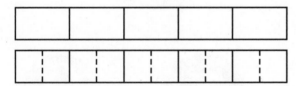

$$\frac{4}{5} = \frac{4 \times \boxed{}}{5 \times \boxed{}} = \frac{8}{10}$$

6. $\frac{9}{12}$ and $\frac{3}{4}$

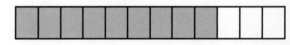

$$\frac{9}{12} = \frac{9 \div \boxed{}}{12 \div \boxed{}} = \frac{3}{4}$$

Complete.

7. $\frac{3}{8} = \frac{3 \times \boxed{}}{8 \times \boxed{}} = \frac{15}{\boxed{}}$

8. $\frac{8}{12} = \frac{8 \div \boxed{}}{12 \div \boxed{}} = \frac{2}{\boxed{}}$

9. Compare. Write >, <, or = in the $\bigcirc$.

$\frac{1}{5} \bigcirc \frac{1}{4}$

Use the spinner to answer exercises 10a. and 10b.

10. **a.** Describe the probability of spinning red on the spinner using one of these words: likely, unlikely, equally likely, certain, or impossible.

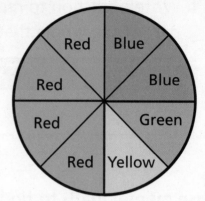

_____

b. Write the probability of spinning blue.

_____ out of _____ or _____

Complete.

11. **a.** Suppose you pull a marble out of the bag 20 times and return it to the bag each time. Which color marble do you predict will be pulled out most often?

_____

b. What are all the possible outcomes when you toss 2 coins? Use H for heads and T for tails to make an organized list.

Write each fraction as a decimal or vice versa.

12. **a.** $\frac{3}{10} =$ _____   **b.** $\frac{42}{100} =$ _____   **c.** $0.65 =$ _____   **d.** $0.5 =$ _____

Write an equivalent decimal.

13. **a.** $0.7 =$ _____   **b.** $0.1 =$ _____

Compare. Write >, <, or =.

14. **a.** $\$0.75 \bigcirc \$0.95$ **b.** $0.6 \bigcirc 0.25$

15. Write the answer with a remainder and as a mixed number.

$6\overline{)38}$

Write the mixed number or improper fraction.

16. $\frac{15}{4} =$ _____   17. $2\frac{7}{8} =$ _____

Add or subtract.

18. $\frac{2}{7} + \frac{3}{7} =$ _____   19. $\frac{6}{9} - \frac{3}{9} =$ _____

Add or subtract. Use the fraction strips to help you.

20. $\frac{1}{6} + \frac{3}{12} =$ _____   21. $\frac{2}{3} - \frac{4}{9} =$ _____

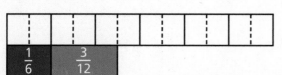   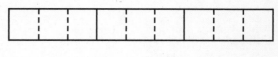

22. Use the bar graph to fill in the blanks.

Vanessa has _____ as many cousins as Andrew.

Andrew has _____ as many cousins as Vanessa.

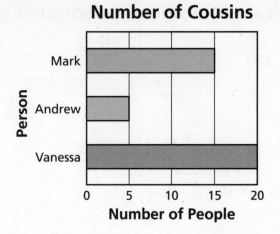

Number of Cousins

Solve.

23. Harris has 41 books. Each shelf in his bookshelf holds 6 books. How many shelves does he need to hold all his books?

_____

24. A store has 63 caps. $\frac{2}{9}$ of the caps are blue. How many blue caps does the store have?

_____

25. Extended Response Use the circle graph to answer the question.

A bakery made 36 batches of cookies in all. How many batches of coconut cookies were made?

Batches of Cookies Baked

_____

Explain how you found your answer.

_____

_____

_____

Name _____ **Date** _____

Class Activity

Vocabulary
net
cube

▶Make a Cube

Cut around the outside of the first **net**. Fold to make a **cube**. Which of the other two nets will make a **cube**? Cut out the nets to test your prediction.

1.
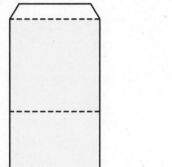

2.
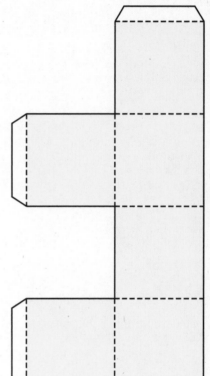

3.
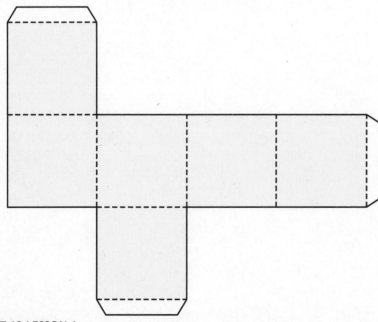

Explore Cubes

▶Identify Cube Nets

Circle the nets that you think will form a cube. Cut out the ones you circled and test your predictions.

4.

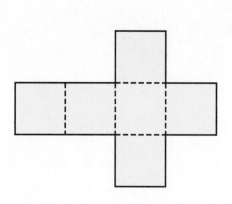

5.

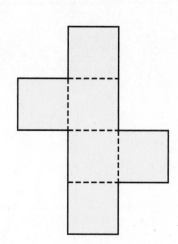

6.

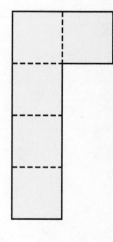

7.

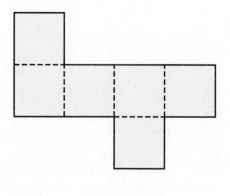

8.

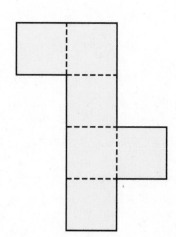

9.

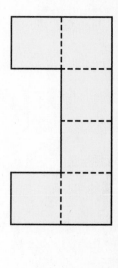

Name _____ **Date** _____

▶ **Create a Cube Net**

10. Draw a net that will form a cube when it is folded.
Then, cut it out and form the cube.

Explore Cubes

Dear Family,

Your child is exploring three-dimensional or solid figures.

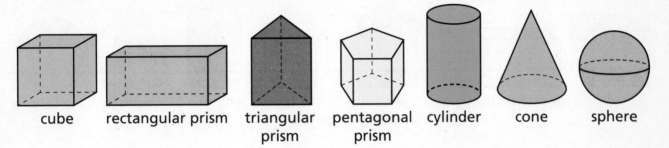

cube   rectangular prism   triangular prism   pentagonal prism   cylinder   cone   sphere

Your child will be making most of these solid figures by cutting out, folding, and taping a two-dimensional net of the object. This is a net for a triangular prism.

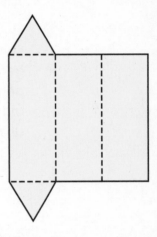

At home, point out different solid figures and discuss them with your child. Ask questions, such as: What is the name of that solid figure? What do you think it would look like from the side, top, back, or front? How is it different from another solid figure?

Encourage your child to build solid figures from cubes, clay, or folded paper.

When you are shopping with your child, discuss the different solid figures used for packaging. Ask your child to consider why particular solid figures are used for certain products.

If you have any questions or comments, please call or write to me.

Sincerely,
Your child's teacher

Estimada familia:

Su niño está explorando figuras tridimensionales o cuerpos geométricos.

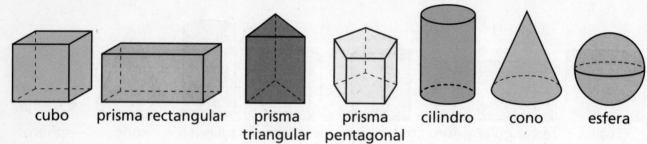

| cubo | prisma rectangular | prisma triangular | prisma pentagonal | cilindro | cono | esfera |

Su niño va a construir estos cuerpos geométricos cortando, doblando y pegando con cinta adhesiva una red bidimensional del objeto. Ésta es una red para un prisma triangular.

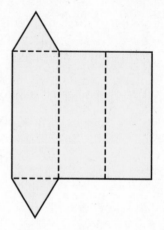

En casa señale diferentes cuerpos geométricos y coméntelos con su niño. Hágale preguntas como: ¿Cómo se llama este cuerpo geométrico? ¿Cómo crees que se vería desde el lado, desde arriba, desde atrás o desde adelante? ¿Cómo se diferencia de otro cuerpo geométrico?

Anime a su niño a que construya cuerpos geométricos usando cubos, arcilla o papel doblando.

Cuando uaya de compras con su niño, comente con él o con ella los distintos cuerpos geométricos que se usan para los envases. Pídale que piense por qué se usan determinados cuerpos geométricos para ciertos productos.

Si tiene alguna duda o comentario, por favor comuníquese conmigo.

Atentamente,
El maestro de su niño

Explore Cubes

►Cube Models From Drawings

Use cubes to build a model from each drawing.

1.

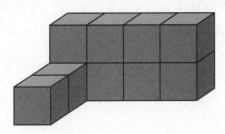

2.

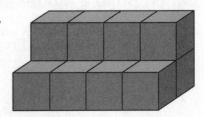

3.

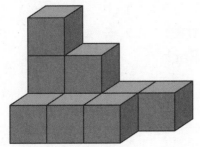

4.

5.

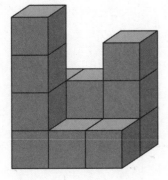

6.

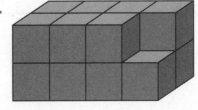

▶ **Views of Three-Dimensional Objects**

7. Label the front, back, left, and right edges of a sheet of paper. Build a model to match the picture.

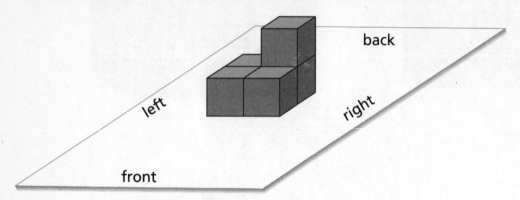

8. Using your model, label the drawings below as the *front, back, right,* or *left* views of the building. Each drawing will have two labels.

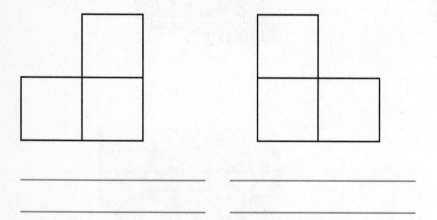

_____   _____
_____   _____

9. Draw the top view of the model from exercise 7.

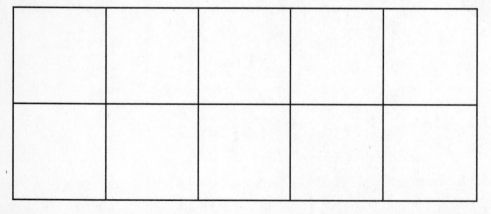

Two-Dimensional Pictures of Three-Dimensional Buildings

10. Build a model to match the drawing below. Place it on a sheet of paper with edges labeled *front, back, right,* and *left.*

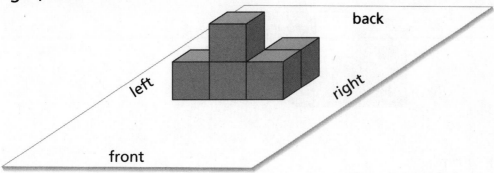

back

left

right

front

11. Using your model, label the views below as *front, back, right,* or *left.* One drawing will have two labels.

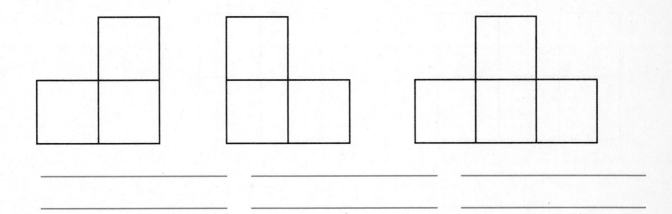

_____   _____   _____

_____   _____   _____

12. Draw the top view of the model from exercise 10.

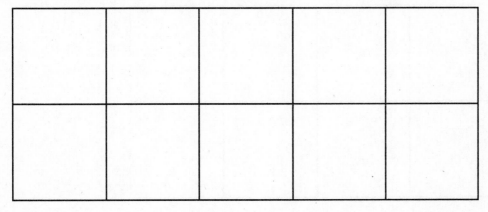

13. Build a model from the drawing below and place it on a sheet of paper with edges labeled *front, back, right,* and *left.*

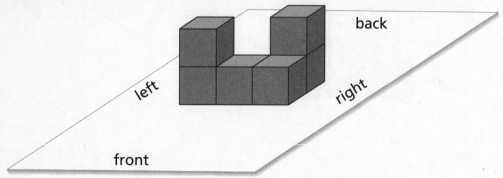

14. Using your model, label the views below as *front, back, left,* or *right.* Each drawing will have two labels.

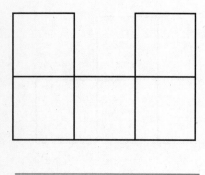

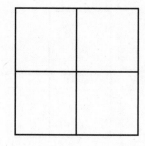

_____

_____

15. Draw the top view of the model from exercise 13.

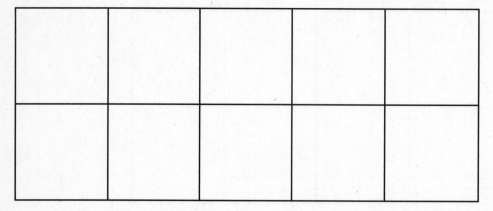

Two-Dimensional Pictures of Three-Dimensional Buildings

►Make Models From Views

Each exercise shows three views of the same model.

Use the views to build a model on a sheet of paper with edges labeled *front, back, right*, and *left*. Compare your model with your partner's.

16.

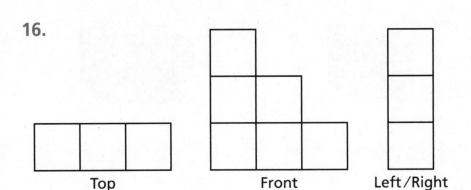

Top   Front   Left/Right

17.

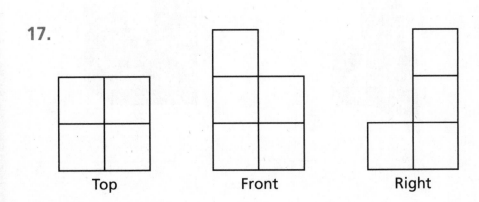

Top   Front   Right

Going Further

►Volume of 3-D Objects

The **volume** of a three-dimensional figure is the number of cubic units that fit inside it.

Find the volume of each figure in cubic units. Build them with cubes if you need to do so.

1 cubic unit

1.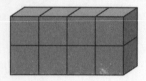

_____

2.

_____

3.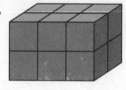

_____

4.

_____

5.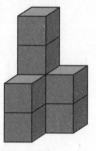

_____

6.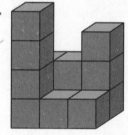

_____

▶ Prism Nets

Cut out each net and form the solid figure.

1.

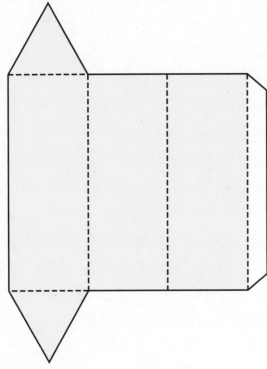

2.

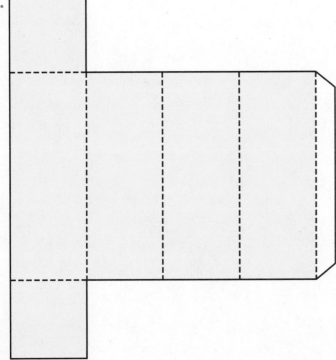

Explore Prisms, Cylinders, and Square Pyramids

Cut out each net and form the solid figure.

3.

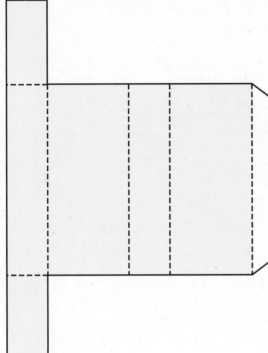

4.

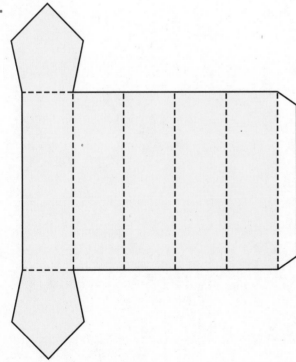

Explore Prisms, Cylinders, and Square Pyramids

►Cylinder Net

Cut out each net and form the solid figure.

5.

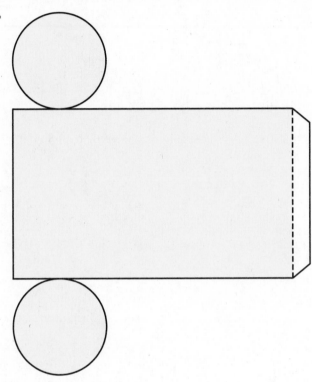

►Square Pyramid Net

6.

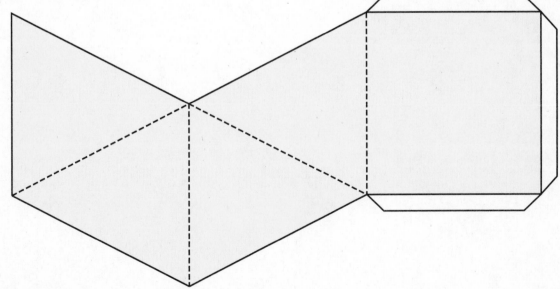

Explore Prisms, Cylinders, and Square Pyramids

▶ **Build a Cone**

Cut out the net and form the solid figure.

1.

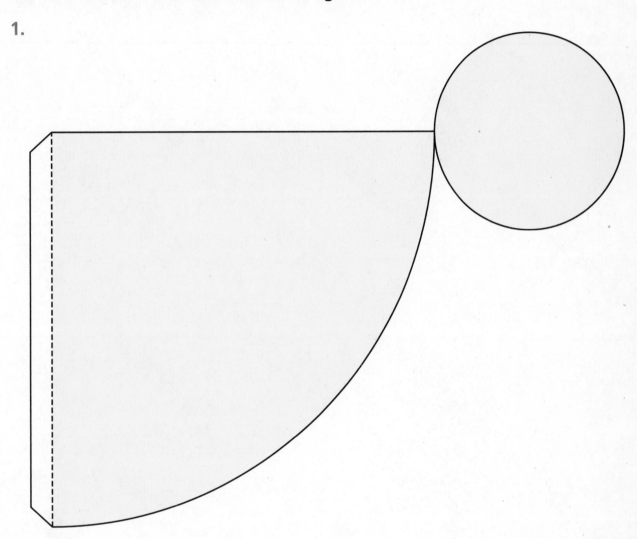

Vocabulary
edge   face
vertex   vertices

► **Sort 3-D Figures**

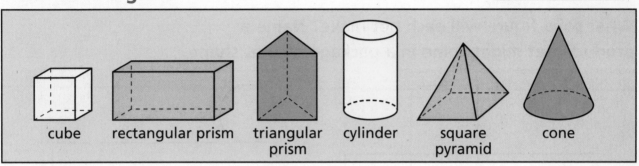

cube   rectangular prism   triangular prism   cylinder   square pyramid   cone

Use the figures above to complete exercises 2–3. Use the words edge, face, and vertex (or vertices).

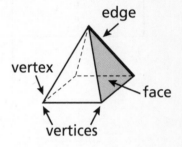

edge

vertex

face

vertices

2. Choose your own sorting rule to sort the solid figures shown into two groups.

My sorting rule is _____

_____

The figures in one group are _____

_____

The figures in the other group are _____

_____

3. Choose a different sorting rule to sort the solid figures shown into two groups.

My sorting rule is _____

_____

The figures in one group are _____

_____

The figures in the other group are _____

_____

▶ Packages

**What solid figure will each net make? Name a
product that might come in a package of that shape.**

4.

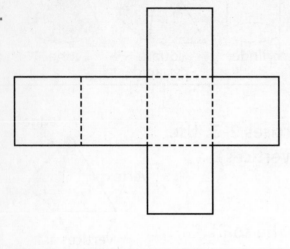

_____

5.

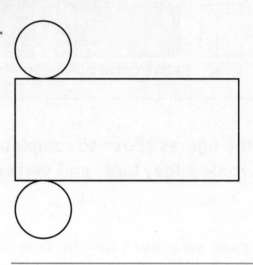

_____

6.

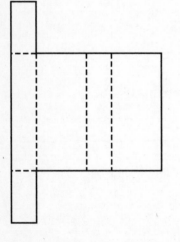

_____

7.

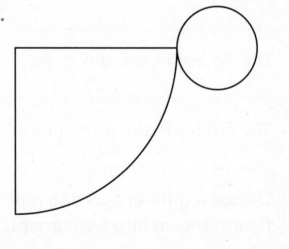

_____

8. Choose a product and design a package for it. You can
   copy one of the nets above onto inch grid paper or
   create your own net for your package. Include your
   product's name and information on the net, color it,
   and then fold it to create your package.

Explore Cones

Class Activity

▶ Characteristics of a Circle

Vocabulary
circle
radius
diameter
circumference

1. Place a pencil inside one end of a paper clip. Hold the pencil point in place on a sheet of paper. Place another pencil inside the other end of the paper clip. Ask a partner to hold your paper still while you draw a **circle** by moving the second pencil.

2. Draw and label a **radius** on your circle.

3. How does the length of the radius compare to the length of the paper clip?

   _____

4. Draw and label a **diameter** on your circle.

5. How does the length of the diameter compare to the length of the paper clip?

   _____

   _____

6. Find the **circumference** of this circle. Describe your method.

   _____

   _____

   _____

   _____

► **Characteristics of a Sphere**

This is a **sphere**.

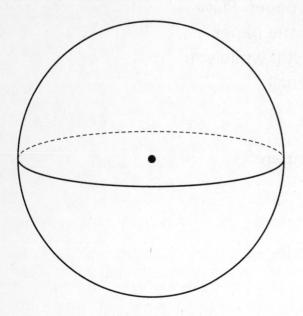

7. How is a sphere similar to a circle?

_____

_____

_____

8. How is a sphere different from a circle?

_____

_____

9. Draw and label a radius on the sphere.

10. Draw and label a diameter on the sphere.

1. Draw a net that will form a cube when folded.

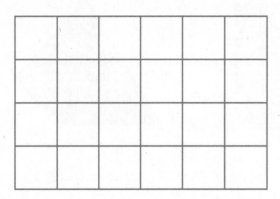

2. Study the model below. Draw the front, back, right, left, and top views.

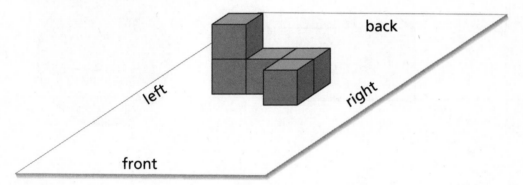

_____ _____ _____

_____   _____

Name the solid figure.

3.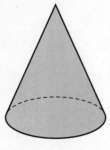

_____

4.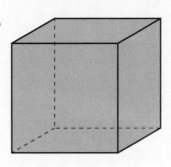

_____

5.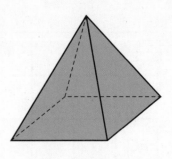

_____

6.

_____

7.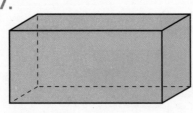

_____

8.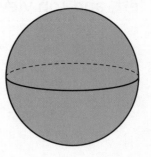

_____

9. Name the solid figure that the net will form.

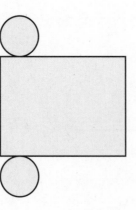

_____

10. Extended Response
Name and describe this prism. Tell what you know about its faces, edges, and vertices.

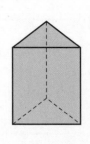

_____

_____

_____

_____

_____

Class Activity

Vocabulary

inch (in.)

▶ **Estimate and Measure Length**

Estimate the length of each line segment in inches.
Then measure it to the nearest inch.

inch

1. _____

Estimate: _____   Actual: _____

2. _____

Estimate: _____   Actual: _____

Estimate the length of each line segment in inches.
Then measure it to the nearest $\frac{1}{2}$ inch.

3. _____

Estimate: _____   Actual: _____

4. _____

Estimate: _____   Actual: _____

Estimate the length of each line segment in inches.
Then measure it to the nearest $\frac{1}{4}$ inch.

5. _____

Estimate: _____   Actual: _____

6. _____

Estimate: _____   Actual: _____

▶ Draw Line Segments

Draw a line segment that has the given length.

7. 5 inches

8. $4\frac{1}{2}$ inches

9. $4\frac{3}{4}$ inches

10. $3\frac{1}{4}$ inches

11. 2 inches

12. $1\frac{1}{4}$ inches

13. $1\frac{1}{2}$ inches

14. $3\frac{3}{4}$ inches

15. Draw a rectangle that is 1 inch wide and 3 inches long.

Dear Family,

In this unit, students explore ways to measure things using the customary and metric systems of measurement.

The units of measurement we will be working with include:

U.S. Customary System

Length
1 foot (ft) = 12 inches (in.) 1 yard (yd) = 3 feet (ft) 1 mile (mi) = 5,280 feet (ft)
Capacity
1 cup (c) = 8 fluid ounces (oz) 1 pint (pt) = 2 cups (c) 1 quart (qt) = 2 pints (pt) 1 gallon (gal) = 4 quarts (qt)
Weight
1 pound (lb) = 16 ounces (oz)

Metric System

Length
1 meter (m) = 10 decimeters (dm) 1 meter (m) = 100 centimeters (cm) 1 decimeter (dm) = 10 centimeters (cm)
Capacity
1 liter (L) = 1,000 milliliters (mL)
Mass
1 kilogram (kg) = 1,000 grams (g)

Students also read, write, and compare temperatures in degrees Fahrenheit and degrees Celsius.

You can help your child become familiar with these units of measurement by working with measurements together. For example, you might estimate and measure the length of something in inches and convert the measurement to feet. You might use a measuring cup to explore how the cup can be used to fill pints, quarts, or gallons of liquid. From inside, you could read the temperature on an outdoor thermometer and decide if it is hot, warm, cool, or cold outside.

Thank you for helping your child learn important math skills. Please call if you have any questions or comments.

Sincerely,
Your child's teacher

Estimada familia:

En esta unidad los estudiantes descubren cómo medir cosas utilizando tanto el sistema medidas usuales como el sistema métrico decimal.

Las unidades de medida con las que trabajaremos incluirán:

Sistema usual	Sistema métrico decimal
Longitud	**Longitud**
1 pie (pie) = 12 pulgadas (pulg) 1 yarda (yd) = 3 pies (pies) 1 milla (mi) = 5,280 pies (pies)	1 metro (m) = 10 decímetros (dm) 1 metro (m) = 100 centímetros (cm) 1 decímetro (dm) = 10 centímetros (cm)
Capacidad	**Capacidad**
1 taza (taza) = 8 onzas líquidas (oz) 1 pinta (pt) = 2 tazas (tazas) 1 cuarto de galón (ct) = 2 pintas (pt) 1 galón (gal) = 4 cuartos de galón (ct)	1 litro (L) = 1,000 mililitros (mL)
Peso	**Masa**
1 libra (lb) = 16 onzas (oz)	1 kilogramo (kg) = 1,000 gramos (g)

Los estudiantes también leen, escriben y comparan temperaturas en grados Farenheit y en grados centígrados.

Puede ayudar a su niño a que se familiarice con estas unidades métricas trabajando juntos con las medidas. Por ejemplo, pueden estimar y medir la longitud de algo en pulgadas y convertir la medida a pies. Podrían usar una taza de medidas para aprender cómo se pueden llenar pintas, cuartos de galón o galones con la taza y un líquido. Desde el interior de la casa podrían leer la temperatura en un termómetro exterior y decidir si la temperatura exterior es caliente, cálida, fresca o fría.

Gracias por ayudar a su niño a aprender destrezas matemáticas importantes.

Si tiene alguna duda o comentario, por favor comuníquese conmigo.

Atentamente,
El maestro de su niño

Name _____ **Date** _____

▶Convert Customary Units of Length

1 foot (ft) = 12 inches (in.)
1 yard (yd) = 3 ft or 36 in.
1 mile (mi) = 5,280 ft or 1,760 yd

Complete.

1. 1 foot 3 inches = _____ inches

2. 1 yard 3 inches = _____ inches

3. 2 feet 5 inches = _____ inches

4. 1 yard 1 foot = _____ inches

5. 1 yard 9 inches = _____ inches

6. 2 feet 7 inches = _____ inches

7. 1 yard 2 feet = _____ inches

8. 2 feet 11 inches = _____ inches

9. 1 foot 10 inches = _____ inches

10. 2 yards = _____ inches

11. 3 feet = 1 _____

12. 6 feet = _____ yards

13. 27 feet = _____ yards

14. 2 feet = _____ inches

15. 32 feet = _____ yards _____ feet or _____ yards

16. 16 feet = _____ yards _____ foot or _____ yards

17. 29 feet = _____ yards _____ feet or _____ yards

18. 25 feet = _____ yards _____ foot or _____ yards

Solve.

19. Marcus has 27 feet of rope to make rope swings. He needs 6 yards of rope for each swing. How many rope swings can he make? How many feet of rope will be left over?

20. Cassidy has 50 inches of ribbon. She wants to divide it equally among her 6 nieces. How many inches of ribbon can each niece have? Give the answer as a mixed number.

_____

_____

Name _____ **Date** _____

Class Activity

▶ Find Benchmarks

Write the answer.

21. This line segment is 1 **inch** long.
    Put two fingers on the line segment. Then hold up
    your fingers. Write the name of an object that is
    about 1 inch (or two finger widths) long.

    _____

22. One **foot** is equal to 12 inches. Spread both hands
    on a ruler to show 1 foot. Write the name of an
    object that is about 1 foot (or both hands) long.

    _____

23. One **yard** is equal to 3 feet or 36 inches. How
    many 12-inch lengths are in 1 yard? Write the
    name of an object that is about 1 yard long.

    _____

24. One **mile** is 5,280 feet or 1,760 yards. In describing
    a long distance, why would it make sense to use
    miles instead of feet or yards?

    _____

▶ Choose Appropriate Units

**Choose the unit you would use to measure each.
Write _inch_, _foot_, _yard_, or _mile_.**

25. the width of a piece of notebook paper _____

26. the length of a classroom board _____

27. the height of the school _____

28. the distance you travel to school _____

Inches, Feet, and Yards

Vocabulary

centimeter (cm)

►Estimate and Measure Length

**Estimate the length of each line segment in centimeters.
Then measure it to the nearest centimeter.**

├──────┤ 1 cm

1. ├────────────┤

Estimate: _____   Actual: _____

2. ├──────────────────┤

Estimate: _____   Actual: _____

3. ├─────────────────────┤

Estimate: _____   Actual: _____

4. ├────────────────────────────┤

Estimate: _____   Actual: _____

5. ├───────────────────────┤

Estimate: _____   Actual: _____

6. Estimate the length of these items in your
   classroom. Then measure to the nearest centimeter.
   Record your information in the chart.

	Estimate (cm)	Actual (cm)
pair of scissors		
gluestick		
pencil		
marker		

▶ Convert Metric Units of Length

Complete the tables.

7.

m	cm
1	100
2	
	300
	400
5	
	600
7	
8	
	900
	1,000

8.

m	dm
1	10
2	
	30
	40
5	
6	
7	
	80
	90
10	

9.

dm	cm
10	100
20	
	300
40	
50	
	600
	700
80	
	900
	1,000

Compare. Write >, <, or = in the ◯ .

10. 120 cm ◯ 1 m

11. 10 dm ◯ 100 cm

12. 3 m ◯ 3,000 cm

13. 6 m ◯ 600 dm

Centimeters, Decimeters, and Meters

Complete the tables.

14.

cm	dm
10	1
20	
30	
40	
	5
	6
	7
80	
	9
	10

15.

cm	m
100	1
	2
	3
400	
500	
600	
	7
	8
900	
1,000	

16.

dm	m
10	1
20	
	3
	4
50	
	6
70	
80	
	9
	10

Compare. Write >, <, or = in the ◯ .

17. 30 dm ◯ 2 m

18. 200 cm ◯ 2 m

19. 70 cm ◯ 70 dm

20. 1 m ◯ 50 cm

21. 800 cm ◯ 7 m

22. 5 dm ◯ 60 cm

Class Activity

▶ Find Benchmarks

23. This line segment is 1 **centimeter** long.
Use your little finger to show 1
centimeter. Write an object that is
about 1 cm (or your little finger width) long.

_____

24. One **decimeter** is equal to 10 cm. This line
segment is 1 decimeter long. Spread your hand to
show 1 decimeter. Write an object that is about
1 dm (or your hand spread out) long.

_____

25. One **meter** is equal to 100 cm. How many
decimeters are in one meter? Write an object or
distance that is about 1 meter long.

_____

26. One **kilometer** is 1,000 meters. It takes you about
10 minutes to walk a kilometer. Write the name of
a place that is about 1 km from your house.

_____

▶ Choose the Appropriate Unit

**Choose the unit you would use to measure each.
Write *centimeter*, *decimeter*, *meter*, or *kilometer*.**

27. the width of your classroom _____

28. the distance you fly on an airplane _____

29. the length of a pencil _____

30. the length of your fingernail _____

Centimeters, Decimeters, and Meters

▶Estimate and Find the Perimeter

Estimate the perimeter in inches. Then measure each side to the nearest $\frac{1}{4}$ inch and find the perimeter.

1.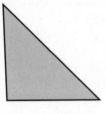

   _____

2.

   _____

3.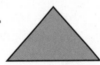

   _____

4.

   _____

5.

   _____

6.

   _____

7.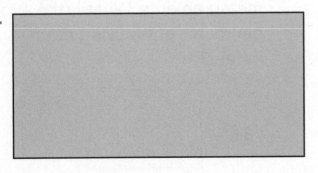

   _____

8.

   _____

Class Activity

▶ Add Customary Units of Length

Add.

9. $3\frac{1}{2}$ inches + 4 inches

_____

10. $8\frac{1}{4}$ inches + $2\frac{1}{4}$ inches

_____

11. $5\frac{1}{2}$ inches + $8\frac{1}{2}$ inches

_____

12. $3\frac{1}{4}$ inches + $2\frac{3}{4}$ inches

_____

13. $4\frac{1}{2}$ inches + $5\frac{1}{4}$ inches

_____

14. $7\frac{1}{4}$ inches + $\frac{1}{2}$ inches

_____

15. $4\frac{1}{2}$ inches + $5\frac{3}{4}$ inches

_____

16. $5\frac{1}{2}$ inches + $5\frac{3}{4}$ inches

_____

17. $3\frac{3}{4}$ inches + $5\frac{3}{8}$ inches

_____

18. $4\frac{5}{8}$ inches + $6\frac{3}{4}$ inches

_____

Solve.

19. Mia wants to make a friendship bracelet. She needs three pieces of string that are each $9\frac{3}{4}$ inches long. How many inches of string does she need in all?

$9\frac{3}{4}$ in. $9\frac{3}{4}$ in. $9\frac{3}{4}$ in.

20. Larry measured his living room. Then he wrote down the measurements. What is the perimeter of his living room in feet?

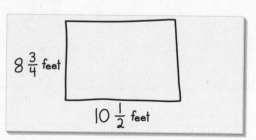

$8\frac{3}{4}$ feet

$10\frac{1}{2}$ feet

_____

Add Lengths

Class Activity

Name _____   Date _____

Vocabulary

cup (c)
fluid ounce (fl oz)
quart (qt)   gallon (gal)

▶ **Units of Capacity**

1 cup = 8 fluid ounces   4 cups  = 1 quart

2 cups = 1 pint   4 quarts = 1 gallon

Solve.

1. Regina drank 2 cups of milk. Rex drank 8 fluid ounces of milk. Who drank more milk?

   _____

2. Fran spilled a half-gallon of water. Mark spilled 3 quarts. Who spilled more water?

   _____

3. Would you rather have a pint and a half of your favorite drink or 4 cups?

   _____

4. Would you rather have a cup or a fourth of a pint of a drink you don't like?

   _____

5. There are 2 quarts of tomato juice in the refrigerator. Mrs. Chavez needs $\frac{3}{4}$ of a gallon to make a stew. Does she have enough? Explain.

   _____

   _____

6. Juana has a 12-cup punch bowl. She uses a 1-quart container to fill it. How many times must she pour a quart into the bowl to fill it? Explain.

   _____

   _____

▶ Convert Units of Capacity

Complete the table.

1 cup (c) = 8 fluid ounces (fl oz)
2 cups (c) = 1 pint (pt)
4 cups (c) = 1 quart (qt)
16 cups (c) = 1 gallon (gal)

	Number of cups	Number of pints	Number of quarts	Number of half-gallons	Number of gallons
Cup					
Pint					
Quart					
Half-Gallon					
Gallon					

Complete.

7. 8 cups = _____ pints

8. $\frac{1}{2}$ cup = _____ fluid ounces

9. 9 pints = _____ quarts

10. _____ pints = 18 quarts

11. _____ quarts = 4 gallons

12. 8 quarts = _____ gallons

13. 16 fluid ounces = 1 _____

14. 8 pints = 1 _____

15. _____ cups = 3 pints

16. 5 pints = _____ quarts

17. _____ fluid ounces = $\frac{1}{2}$ gallon

18. _____ quarts = $8\frac{1}{4}$ gallons

Customary Units of Capacity

▶ **Establish Benchmarks**

Complete.

19. This container holds 1 cup. Write the name of
another container that holds about 1 cup.

_____

20. This container holds 1 pint. Write the name of
another container that holds about 1 pint.

_____

21. This container holds 1 quart. Write the name of
another container that holds about 1 quart.

_____

22. This container holds 1 gallon. Write the name of
another container that holds about 1 gallon.

_____

▶ **Choose Units**

**Choose the best unit to use to measure how much
each item can hold. Write *cup, pint, quart,* or *gallon.***

23. a carton of heavy cream

_____

24. a swimming pool

_____

25. a flower vase

_____

26. a wash tub

_____

27. **Math Journal** Think of a container. Choose the
unit you would use to measure its capacity. Draw
the container and write the name of the unit you
chose. Explain why you chose that unit.

Class Activity

Name _____ **Date** _____

▶Estimate Customary Units of Capacity

Ring the better estimate.

28.

2 cups

2 quarts

29.

5 gallons

5 cups

30.

1 pint

1 gallon

31.

1 cup

1 pint

32.

1 cup

1 gallon

33.

5 gallon

30 gallon

Solve.

34. Jamie makes a shopping list for a picnic with his four friends. He estimates that he'll need a pint of lemonade for the group to drink. Do you think his estimate is reasonable? Explain.

_____

_____

_____

Class Activity

▶ Convert Metric Units of Capacity

> **1 liter (L) = 1,000 milliliters (mL)**

Complete.

1. 2 L = _____ mL

2. 15,000 mL = _____ L

3. $\frac{1}{2}$ L = _____ mL

4. _____ L = 250 mL

5. _____ L = 4,000 mL

6. 4,000 mL = _____ L

▶ Benchmarks for a Liter and a Milliliter

Write the answer.

7. This bottle holds 1 **liter**.

Name another container that
holds about 1 liter.

_____

8. This eyedropper holds 1 **milliliter**.

Name another container that
holds about 1 milliliter.

_____

▶ Choose the Appropriate Unit

**Choose the unit you would use to measure the
capacity of each. Write *mL* or *L*.**

9. a kitchen sink _____

10. a soup spoon _____

11. a teacup _____

12. a washing machine _____

Circle the better estimate.

13. a juice container   1 L   1 mL

14. a bowl of soup   500 L   500 mL

Class Activity

▶ Solve Problems Involving Capacity

Solve.

15. Diane has 39 cups of lemonade to divide equally among 4 tables. How much lemonade should she put at each table?

16. A recipe calls for 3 pints of milk. How many times must you fill a 1-cup measuring cup to make 3 pints?

17. Mr. Valle made 26 cups of barbeque sauce. He wants to divide it equally among 3 friends. How much sauce will each friend get?

18. Rebecca has 33 cups of ice. Each pitcher of iced tea needs 4 cups of ice. How many pitchers can Rebecca fill? How much ice will be left over?

19. One bottle of water has a red label and holds 2 liters. Another bottle of water has a blue label and holds 1,500 milliliters. What color is the label on the larger bottle?

20. Camilla poured 2,300 milliliters of punch into a punch bowl. Then José poured 3 more liters of punch into the bowl. How many milliliters of punch are in the bowl altogether?

21. A bowl of punch has 2L of lemon-lime soda and 600 mL of lemonade. How many more mL of lemon-lime soda does the punch have?

22. A pudding recipe makes 6 cups of pudding. Will a 1-quart container be large enough to hold the pudding? Why or why not?

23. Would you rather have 500 milliliters of your favorite drink or $\frac{1}{4}$ liter?

24. A bottle holds 750 mL. How many liters will 2 bottles hold?

Class Activity

Name _____   Date _____

▶ Use Improper Fractions and Mixed Numbers in Measurements

Write the improper fraction or mixed number for each measurement.

1. $\frac{7}{2}$ c = _____

2. $\frac{9}{5}$ L = _____

3. $\frac{18}{4}$ m = _____

4. $1\frac{3}{8}$ qt = _____

5. $1\frac{3}{4}$ ft = _____

6. $3\frac{2}{3}$ gal = _____

7. $4\frac{1}{2}$ in. = _____

8. $\frac{16}{7}$ pt = _____

9. $3\frac{7}{8}$ c = _____

10. $2\frac{5}{6}$ mi = _____

11. $3\frac{1}{3}$ yd = _____

12. $\frac{19}{12}$ ml = _____

13. $\frac{17}{9}$ km = _____

14. $2\frac{1}{4}$ in. = _____

15. $\frac{21}{5}$ qt = _____

▶Fractions as Lengths

Write the length of each line segment using a fraction.

16.

_____

17.

_____

18.

_____

**Write the length of each line segment using
an improper fraction and a mixed number.**

19.

_____

20.

_____

21.

_____

22.

_____

Improper Fractions and Mixed Numbers in Measurements

▶Review Measurement Equivalencies

Complete.

1.

Inches	Feet
12	1
1	$\frac{1}{12}$
2	
4	

2.

Feet	Yards
	1
1	
2	
4	

3.

cm	m
	1
1	
87	
158	

4.

Cup	Pint
	1
1	
	2
3	

5.

Pint	Quart
	1
1	
6	
	$1\frac{1}{2}$

6.

Quart	Gallon
4	1
1	
2	
	$1\frac{1}{2}$

7. 1,500 mL = _____

8. 7L = _____

9. 16 cups = _____ pints = _____ quarts = 1 gallon

10. 1 cup = _____ pint = _____ quart = _____ gallon

11. 6 c = _____ pt = _____ qt = _____ gal

12. 48 c = _____ pt = _____ qt = _____ gal

13. Math Journal Seth wants to make a rectangular garden. He has 20 feet of fence. Draw two possible rectangular gardens that Seth could make with the fence. Label the gardens in both feet and inches.

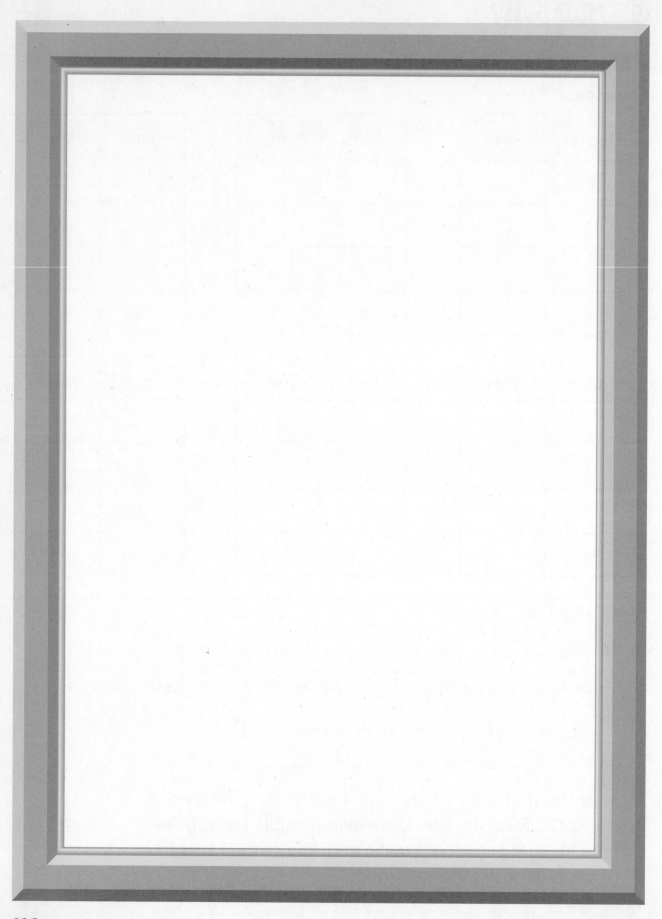

Measurement Equivalencies and Fractions

Class Activity

Name _____ **Date** _____

Vocabulary

pound (lb)
ounce (oz)

▶ Ounces or Pounds

Complete.

1.

Ounces	Pounds
16	1
1	
	2
	3
8	
4	

2.

Pounds	Ounces
$1\frac{1}{2}$	
$2\frac{3}{4}$	
4	
	68
$4\frac{1}{2}$	
	76

3. 2 lb = _____ oz

4. 60 oz = _____ lb

5. 10 lb = _____ oz

6. _____ lb = 12 oz

7. 2 oz = _____ lb

8. 40 oz = _____ lb

▶ Establish Benchmarks for a Pound and an Ounce

9. This weighs about 1 **ounce**.

Name another item that weighs about 1 ounce.

_____

10. This weighs about 1 **pound**.

Name another item that weighs about 1 pound.

_____

▶ Choose the Appropriate Unit

Choose the unit you would use to measure the weight of each. Write *pound* or *ounce*.

11. a backpack full of books

_____

12. a couch

_____

13. a peanut

_____

14. a pencil

_____

Circle the better estimate.

15. a student desk	3 lb	30 lb
16. a television	20 oz	20 lb
17. a hamster	5 oz	5 lb
18. a slice of cheese	1 lb	1 oz

Solve.

19. Kiko bought 2 pounds of peaches, 8 ounces of cherries, 12 ounces of plums, and $1\frac{1}{4}$ pounds of apples. What was the total weight of her purchases?

_____

_____

20. A pound of potatoes was used to make some soup. If the soup is divided evenly among 8 people, how many ounces of potatoes will each person get?

_____

21. Would you rather have a pound and a half of your favorite nuts or 20 ounces?

_____

22. Gregory bought $1\frac{1}{4}$ pounds of nails at 10¢ an ounce. How much did he pay?

_____

Class Activity

Name _____ Date _____

Vocabulary
gram (g)
kilogram (kg)

▶ Grams and Kilograms

Complete.

23.

Grams	Kilograms
1,000	1
1	
	2
	3
500	
40	

24.

Kilograms	Grams
$1\frac{1}{2}$	
$\frac{200}{1,000}$	
	250
$5\frac{3}{4}$	
6	
$6\frac{1}{2}$	6,500

25. 2 kg = _____ g

26. 750 g = _____ kg

27. 10 kg = _____ g

28. _____ kg = 500 g

▶ Benchmarks for a Gram and a Kilogram

Write the answer.

29. A paper clip has a mass of about 1 **gram**.

Name another item with a mass of about 1 gram.

_____

30. A math book has a mass of about 1 **kilogram**.

Name another item with a mass of about 1 kilogram.

_____

▶Choose the Appropriate Unit

Choose the unit you would use to measure the mass of each. Write *gram* or *kilogram*.

31. an elephant

_____

32. a crayon

_____

33. a stamp

_____

34. a dog

_____

Circle the better estimate.

35. a pair of sunglasses   150 g   150 kg

36. a horse   6 kg   600 kg

37. a watermelon   40 g   4 kg

38. a quarter   500 g   5 g

Solve.

39. The mass of a small penguin is 1 kilogram 800 grams. How many grams less than 2 kilograms is that?

_____

40. Would you rather have $\frac{1}{2}$ kilogram or 400 grams of your favorite candy?

_____

41. Rolls of coins are sometimes weighed to check how many are inside. A penny weighs about 3 g. About how many grams would a dollar's worth of pennies weigh?

_____

42. Jenna wants to put 200 grams of peanuts in each of 5 small cups for party favors. Would a 1-kg bag of peanuts be enough to fill the cups? Explain.

_____

_____

_____

► **Choose the Better Estimate**

Ring the better estimate.

43.

200 grams

200 kilograms

44.

10 kilograms

10 grams

45.

1 ounce

1 pound

46.

100 pounds

10 ounces

47.

100 pounds

1 ton

48.

1 kilogram

10 kilograms

Solve.

49. Suzie estimated the weights of objects and ordered them by the estimates of their weights. She explained that estimating them was easy since the smallest objects weighed the least and the largest objects weighed the most. Do you agree with Suzie?

_____

_____

Name _____ **Date** _____

Going Further

▶Add and Subtract Measurements

Dear Math Students,

Today my teacher asked me to add 2 feet
6 inches and 3 feet 8 inches. Here is how
I solved the problem. Is my calculation right?

> 2 ft 6 in.
> +3 ft 8 in.
> ‾‾‾‾‾‾‾‾‾‾
> 6 ft 4 in.

If not, please correct my work and explain below.
Thank you,
The Puzzled Penguin

50. _____

_____

Solve.

51.　3 ft 5 in.
　+ 4 ft 9 in.

52.　4 yd 1 ft
　− 1 yd 2 ft

53.　6 lb 8 oz
　+ 3 lb 7 oz

54.　3 pt 1 c
　+ 5 pt 1 c

55.　6 h 20 min
　− 4 h 30 min

56.　5 days 17 h
　+ 3 days 12 h

57. Carlie jumped 48 dm, 340 cm and 4 m on her third triple jump. What is the total distance she jumped in centimeters?

58. Aaron made 4 lb of potato salad. He put 2 lb 6 oz in take-out containers. How much potato salad is left?

_____

_____

　　　　　　　　Customary Units of Weight and Mass

Class Activity

►Temperature in Fahrenheit

Circle the better estimate of the temperature.

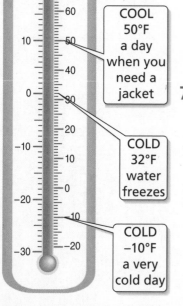

1. **2.** **3.**

20°F   80°F   32°F   84°F   0°F   53°F

Write the temperature using °F. Then write *hot,*
***warm, cool,* or *cold* to describe the temperature.**

4. **5.** **6.**

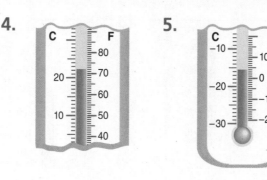

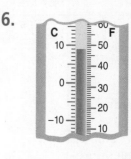

_____   _____   _____

7. **8.** **9.**

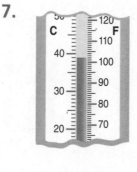

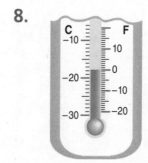

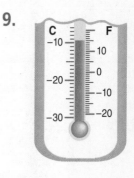

_____   _____   _____

Class Activity

Name _____ **Date** _____

▶ Temperature in Celsius

Circle the better estimate of the temperature.

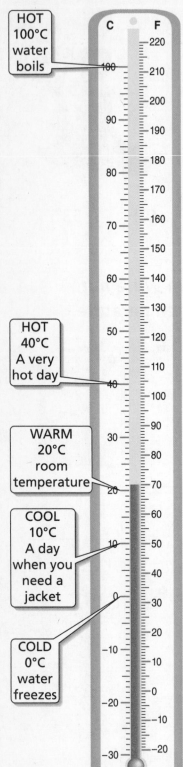

HOT
100°C
water
boils

HOT
40°C
A very
hot day

WARM
20°C
room
temperature

COOL
10°C
A day
when you
need a
jacket

COLD
0°C
water
freezes

10.

50°C   11°C

11.

30°C   100°C

12.

22°C   0°C

Write the temperature using °C. Then write *hot, warm, cool,* or *cold* to describe the temperature.

13.

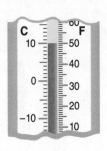

_____

14.

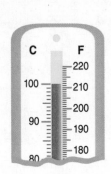

_____

15.

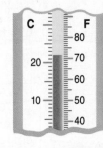

_____

16.

_____

17.

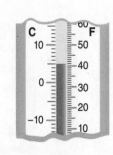

_____

18.

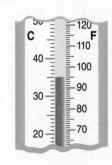

_____

Temperature

Name _____ **Date** _____

Class Activity

► **Math and Science**

Bees store the honey they make in a structure called honeycomb. The bees need the honey that is stored for food during the winter. The best thing for the bees is to have as much space as possible to store the honey.

1. Cover a piece of paper with circular counters. Cover the same size piece of paper with pattern block hexagons. Do the circles cover the page completely?

_____

   Do the hexagons cover the page completely?

_____

2. The honeycomb is made out of hexagons. Why does the hexagon work better for the bees than the circle?

_____

_____

_____

3. You can surround 1 hexagon with 6 hexagons and there won't be any holes. Use pattern blocks to support or disprove the statements.

_____

_____

Name _____ **Date** _____

Class Activity

▶ Shadows

4. If you measured the shadow of a yardstick at different times of the day, do you think the shadow would always be the same length or would it be different? Make a prediction.

_____

_____

5. Measure the length of the shadow of a yardstick at four different times of the day. Put the yardstick at the same spot each time. Record the shadow lengths in the table below.

Time of Day	Length of Shadow of Yardstick

6. On a separate piece of paper, make a bar graph that shows the length of the shadow at different times of the day.

7. Write about what you found out. Compare what you found out to what you predicted in exercise 4.

_____

_____

_____

_____

Use Mathematical Processes

1. Estimate the length of the line segment in inches.
   Then measure it to the nearest $\frac{1}{4}$ inch.

   Estimate: _____

   Actual: _____

2. Estimate the length of the line segment
   to the nearest centimeter. Then measure
   it to the nearest centimeter.

   Estimate: _____

   Actual: _____

Complete.

3. 2 feet 3 inches = _____ inches

4. 24 feet = _____ yards

5. 1 yard 2 feet = _____ inches

6. 2 meters = _____ centimeters

7. 400 centimeters = _____ meters

8. 5 pints = _____ cups

9. 13 quarts = _____ gallons

10. 8 quarts = _____ pints

11. 1 liter = _____ milliliters

12. 24 ounces = _____ pounds

13. 2 pounds = _____ ounces

14. 2,000 grams = _____ kilograms

15. **Ring the better estimate.**

a.

2 gallons

2 cups

b.

12 ounces

12 pounds

c.

30 milliliters

3 liters

16. Write the temperature. Then write *hot, warm, cool,* or *cold* to describe the temperature.

a.

_____ °F _____

b.

_____ °C _____

17. Use the rectangle around 17a.–c. to complete 17a.–c.

a. Estimate the perimeter in inches. _____

b. Find the actual perimeter in inches.

_____

c. Estimate the area in square inches.

_____

Solve.

18. Bert has 56 gallons of water for the pet shop's fish tanks. Each tank holds 6 gallons of water. How many tanks can Bert fill? How much water will be left?

_____

19. A ten-gallon fish tank needs to have half of its water replaced every two weeks. How many quarts of water need to be replaced every two weeks?

_____

20. Extended Response A loaf of bread has 40 slices. Each slice weighs 1 ounce. How many pounds does the loaf of bread weigh? Explain how you found the answer.

_____

_____

Class Activity

▶Read a Map

Each square on the **map** is 1 block. You can travel up, down, right, or left along the lines on the map.

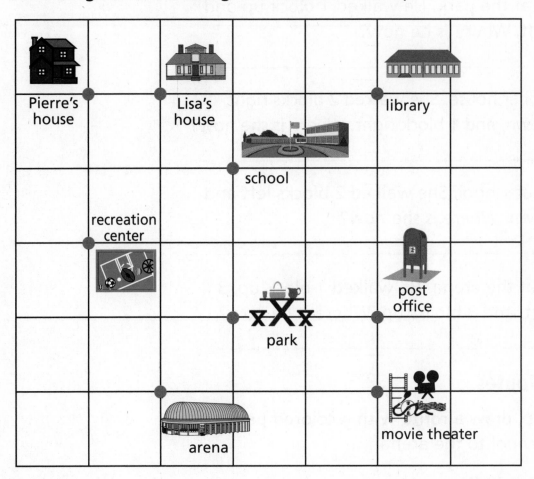

1. How many blocks is the school from the park?

_____

2. How many blocks is the library from the post office?

_____

3. Whose house is closer to the library, Pierre's or Lisa's?

_____

By how much? _____

Class Activity

Vocabulary

route

▶ Follow Directions

Use the map on page 509 to answer the questions.

4. Pierre was at the park. He walked 1 block up and 2 blocks left. Where is he now?

_____

5. Lisa was at her house. She walked 2 blocks right, 3 blocks down, and 1 block right. Where is she now?

_____

6. Sarah was at school. She walked 2 blocks left and 1 block down. Where is she now?

_____

7. Lucio was at the arena. He walked 1 block up, 3 blocks right, and 3 blocks up. Where is he now?

_____

▶ Describe Routes

8. On the map, draw a **route** with a colored pencil from the school to the arena.

9. Describe your route.

_____

10. How many blocks long is your route?

_____

11. On the map, draw another route with a different colored pencil from the school to the arena.

12. Describe your route.

_____

13. Which of your routes is longer?

_____

Class Activity

Name

Date

▶Make a Map

14. Draw a map of an amusement park. Include a
    waterfall, treasure chest, bumper cars, a snack bar,
    and other places such as raging rapids, scrambler,
    pirates cove, or sunken ship. Place each point for
    the place where two grid lines intersect on the map.

►Use Your Map

Use the map you created on page 511 to complete the following.

15. Draw a route on your map with a colored pencil from the snack bar to the bumper cars.

16. Describe this route.

_____

_____

17. Draw a route on your map with a different colored pencil from the snack bar to the water fall.

18. Describe this route.

_____

_____

19. Which place is further from the snack bar, the bumper cars or the waterfall?

_____

Choose two places on your map.

20. Name the two places and describe a route from one to the other.

_____

_____

21. Describe a different route from one place to the other.

_____

_____

22. Is the second route longer, shorter, or equal in distance to your first route?

_____

Directions and Maps

Dear Family,

Your child is working on a geometry unit about coordinate grids.

Students first work on grids without number labels. Then they make a map by adding features (places or objects) where two grid lines intersect. They describe routes on the map as up, down, right, and left in blocks or units.

Students then progress to coordinate grids — grids with number labels for each horizontal and vertical line. They describe locations on grids using ordered pairs. For example, this coordinate grid shows the point (2, 3). The first number in the ordered pair shows how far to the right the point is from 0. The second number shows how far up the point is from 0.

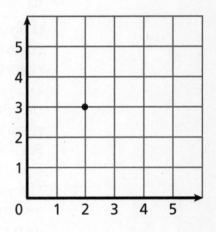

In the last lesson, students draw triangles and quadrilaterals on coordinate grids. They also use grid lines to measure the length of line segments and to draw rectangles from specific descriptions. The rectangle shown here is a possible response to the following description: The width of the rectangle is 3 units shorter than its length.

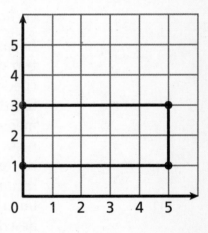

If you have any questions or comments, please call or write to me.

Sincerely,
Your child's teacher

Estimada familia:

Su niño está trabajando en una unidad de geometría sobre las cuadrículas de coordenadas.

Al principio, los estudiantes trabajan con cuadrículas que no están rotuladas con números. Agregan puntos (que representan lugares u objetos) donde se cruzan dos rectas para hacer un mapa. Describen las rutas en el mapa en términos de bloques o unidades hacia arriba, hacia abajo, hacia la derecha o hacia la izquierda.

Luego, los estudiantes usan cuadrículas de coordenadas, o sea, cuadrículas rotuladas con números en la recta horizontal y vertical. Describen ubicaciones en las cuadrículas usando pares ordenados. Por ejemplo, esta cuadrícula de coordenadas muestra el punto (2, 3). El primer número del par ordenado muestra a qué distancia a la derecha de 0 está el punto, y el segundo número muestra a qué distancia vertical está de 0.

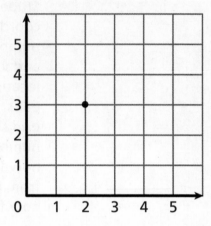

En la última lección los estudiantes trazan triángulos y cuadriláteros en cuadrículas de coordenadas. También usan las rectas de la cuadrícula para medir la longitud de segmentos de recta y trazan rectángulos a partir de descripciones específicas. El rectángulo que se muestra aquí es una respuesta posible a la siguiente descripción: el rectángulo tiene 3 unidades menos de ancho que de largo.

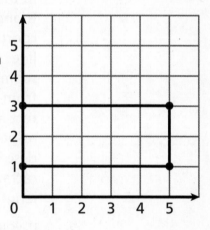

Si tiene alguna duda o pregunta, por favor comuníquese conmigo.

Atentamente,
El maestro de su niño

Class Activity

Vocabulary

ordered pair
coordinate grid

▶ Coordinate Grids

You can use **ordered pairs** to find and name points on a **coordinate grid**.

Hector's Backyard

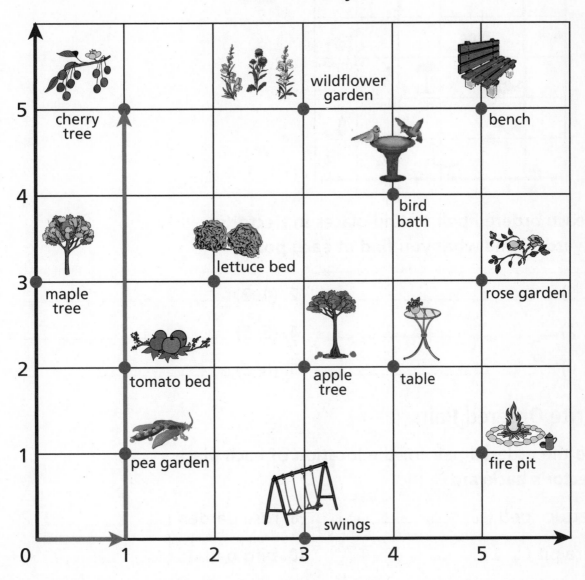

The cherry tree is located at (1, 5). To find (1, 5), start at 0. The first number tells how many spaces to the **right**, so move 1 space to the right. The second number tells how many spaces **up**, so move 5 spaces up.

(right, up)

► **Locate Points**

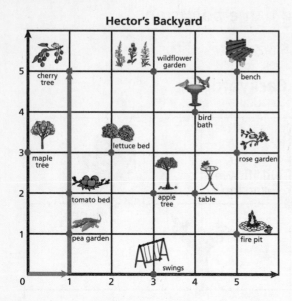

Hector's Backyard

Use each ordered pair to find places in Hector's backyard. Name what you find at each point.

1. (3, 5) _____   2. (4, 2) _____

3. (1, 2) _____   4. (5, 5) _____

5. (3, 0) _____   6. (0, 3) _____

► **Write Ordered Pairs**

Write the ordered pair for the location of each place in Hector's backyard.

7. lettuce bed (_____, _____)   8. rose garden (_____, _____)

9. fire pit (_____, _____)   10. bird bath (_____, _____)

11. apple tree (_____, _____)   12. maple tree (_____, _____)

13. Draw a new place at the intersection of two grid lines on the map of Hector's backyard.
Write the ordered pair for its location. (_____, _____)

▶Solve Problems With Ordered Pairs

Use the coordinate grid below for exercises 14–18.

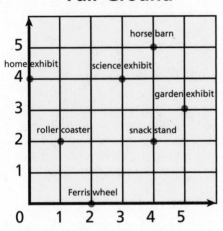

Fair Ground

14. Larry went to the fair with his sister, Marissa. First they went to (1, 2). Where did they go first?

_____

15. Larry and Marissa went to (3, 4). What is located at (3, 4)?

_____

16. In the afternoon, Larry went to the home exhibit and Marissa went to the Ferris wheel. Write the ordered pairs for each location.

    home exhibit (_____, _____)   Ferris wheel (_____, _____)

17. What do the points for the Ferris wheel and home exhibit have in common?

_____

18. Larry said he would meet Marissa at the horse barn at (5, 4). What mistake did he make? What is the correct ordered pair?

_____

Class Activity

▶ Figures on Grids

Use the coordinate grid below for exercises 19–22.

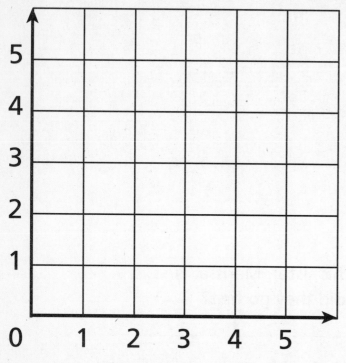

19. Graph each ordered pair. Label the point with the given letter.

   Point *A* (1, 1), Point *B* (1, 4), Point *C* (2, 4), Point *D* (2, 1)

20. Draw a line segment to connect the points in order that you marked for exercise 19. Name the figure you drew.

   _____

21. Graph each ordered pair. Label the point with the given letter.

   Point *E* (3, 3), Point *F* (3, 5), Point *G* (5, 5), Point *H* (5, 3)

22. Draw a line segment to connect the points in order that you marked for exercise 21. Name the figure you drew.

   _____

Locate Points on a Coordinate Grid

Class Activity

▶ Triangles on Coordinate Grids

1. Mark a point on this coordinate grid to form the third vertex of a right triangle. Join the three points with line segments to make a right triangle.

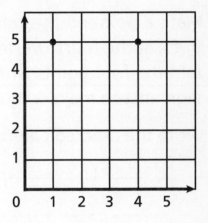

2. Write the ordered pair for each vertex.

   (＿＿, ＿＿) (＿＿, ＿＿) (＿＿, ＿＿)

3. Mark a point on this coordinate grid to form the third vertex of an obtuse triangle. Join the three points to make an obtuse triangle.

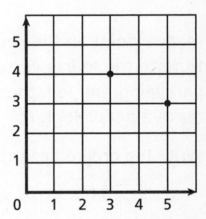

4. Write the ordered pair for each vertex.

   (＿＿, ＿＿) (＿＿, ＿＿) (＿＿, ＿＿)

5. Draw a triangle on this coordinate grid. Place each vertex at the intersection of two grid lines.

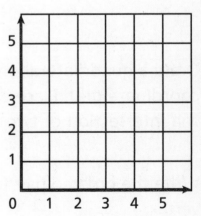

6. Write the ordered pair for each vertex.

   (＿＿, ＿＿) (＿＿, ＿＿) (＿＿, ＿＿)

Class Activity

▶Quadrilaterals on Coordinate Grids

7. Mark a point on this coordinate grid to form the fourth vertex of a square. Join the four points with line segments to make a square.

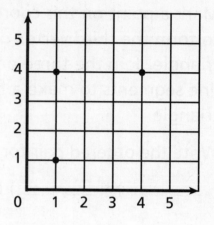

8. Write the ordered pair for each vertex.

(____, ____) (____, ____)

(____, ____) (____, ____)

9. Mark a point on this coordinate grid to form the fourth vertex of a parallelogram. Join the four points to make a parallelogram.

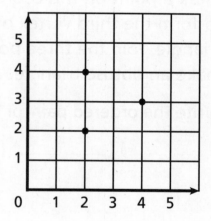

10. Write the ordered pair for each vertex.

(____, ____) (____, ____)

(____, ____) (____, ____)

11. Draw a quadrilateral on this coordinate grid. Place each vertex at the intersection of two grid lines.

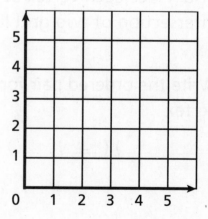

12. Write the ordered pair for each vertex.

(____, ____) (____, ____)

(____, ____) (____, ____)

Class Activity

▶Distance Between Points

The distance between two parallel line segments on a grid is 1 unit.

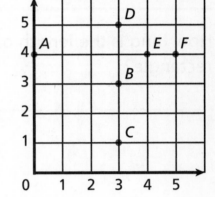

13. Draw a horizontal line segment from A to E. How long is the line segment?

_____

14. Draw a horizontal line segment from E to F. How long is the line segment?

_____

15. How long is the line segment from A to F?

_____

16. Draw a vertical line segment from D to B. How long is the line segment?

_____

17. Draw a vertical line segment from B to C. How long is the line segment?

_____

18. How long is the line segment from D to C?

_____

19. Draw a horizontal line segment with endpoints at the intersection of grid lines.

20. How long is your horizontal line segment?

_____

21. Draw a line segment that is perpendicular to your horizontal line segment with endpoints at the intersection of grid lines.

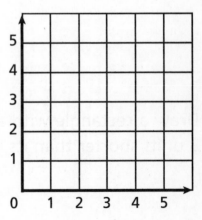

22. How long is your vertical line segment?

_____

Class Activity

▶ Dimensions of Rectangles

23. How long is the width of this rectangle?

_____

24. How long is the length of this rectangle?

_____

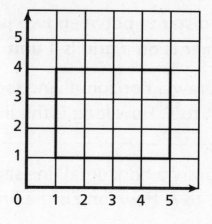

25. Draw a rectangle with a length that is 2 units longer than its width.

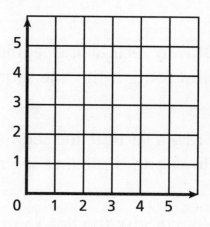

26. Draw a rectangle with a width that is 3 units shorter than its length.

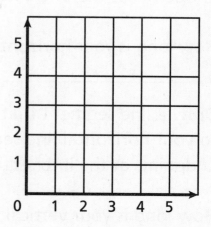

Explore Line Segments and Figures on a Coordinate Grid

Use the coordinate grid below to complete exercises 1–4.

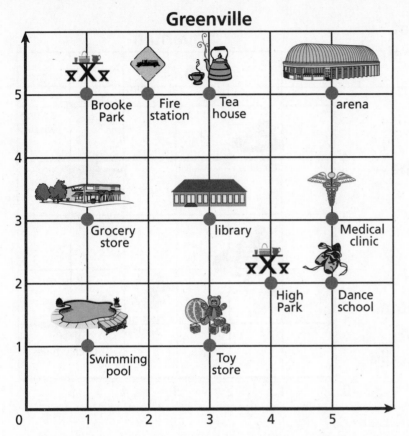

Greenville

1. Lita started at the toy store. She walked 2 blocks right and 1 block up. Where is she?

_____

2. Lyle was at Brooke Park. He walked 1 block down, 3 blocks right, and 2 blocks down. Where is he?

_____

3. Chen was at the arena. He walked 1 block down, 3 blocks left, 3 blocks down, and 1 block left. Where is he?

_____

4. Michaela wants to go from Brooke Park to the Dance school. Describe a route that she can take.

_____

Use the coordinate grid below to complete
exercises 5–10.

**Name the animals you find at
the point for each ordered pair.**

5. (1, 2) _____

6. (5, 0) _____

**Write the ordered pair for the
location of the animals.**

7. Sharks (_____ , _____)

8. Dolphins (_____ , _____)

9. Mato went to the aquarium.
The first place he went to
was at (5, 5). Which place did
he go to first?

_____

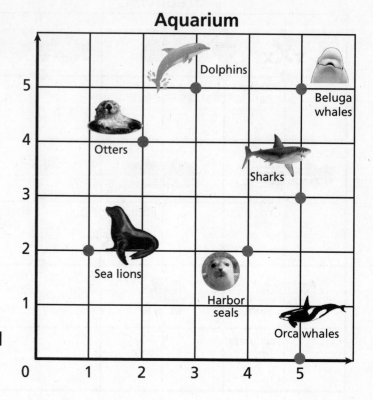

Aquarium

10. **Extended Response** After watching the sea lions being
fed, Mato went to see the otters and the harbor seals.
Write the ordered pair for each animal.

otters (_____ , _____)   harbor seals (_____ , _____)

What is the order of the numbers in an ordered pair?
Why does the order matter? Use the example of the otters
and harbor seals in your explanation.

_____

_____

_____

_____

_____

Test

Name _____ **Date** _____

Class Activity

▶ **Identify Place Value Through Hundred Thousands**

Vocabulary

place value
standard form
word form

To read and write numbers you need to understand **place value**.

1. What are the names of the places of a three-digit number?

_____

Hundreds	Tens	Ones
2	3	5

2. How do we read and write 235 with words?

_____

Hundred Thousands	Ten Thousands	Thousands	Hundreds	Tens	Ones
1	6	8	2	3	5

Write the value of the underlined digit.

3. 1<u>3</u>,456 _____

4. 190,<u>7</u>65 _____

5. <u>8</u>8,763 _____

6. 4,5<u>6</u>7 _____

▶ **Write Numbers Different Ways**

Standard form: 15,678   **Word form**: fifteen thousand, six hundred seventy-eight

Write each number in standard form.

7. six thousand, one hundred eight _____

8. six thousand eight _____

9. one hundred sixty six thousand, eighty _____

Write each number in word form.

10. 17,893 _____

11. 175,635 _____

Class Activity

▶ **Compare and Order Numbers to 10,000**

Discuss the problem below.

Jim has 24 trading cards and Hattie has 42 trading cards. Who has more trading cards? How do you know?

Write greater than (>), less than (<), or equal (=) to make each statement true.

12. 4,008 ◯ 4,108   13. 2,356 ◯ 2,563   14. 8,567 ◯ 9,567

15. 3,989 ◯ 3,899   16. 2,385 ◯ 2,385   17. 3,235 ◯ 2,350

Write each group of numbers in order from greatest to least.

18. 8,456   4,567   4,675   19. 3,465   3,654   3,546

_____   _____

▶ **Add, Subtract, and Estimate with Large Numbers**

Solve using any method. Use estimation to check that your results are reasonable.

20.   73,608
     + 9,729
    _____

21.   33,756
     − 13,897
    _____

22. Bob's town has a population of 13,226 people. Mia's town has 11,867 people. Tani's town has 33,569 people. How many people live in the three towns?

_____

23. How many more people live in Tani's town than Bob's town?

_____

Class Activity

Name _____ **Date** _____

Vocabulary

array
area

▶ Model a Product of Ones

The number of unit squares in an **array** of connected unit squares is the **area** of the rectangle formed by the squares. We sometimes just show the measurement of length and width.

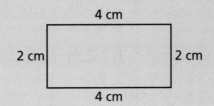

You can draw a rectangle for any multiplication. In the real world, we use multiplication for finding both sizes of arrays and areas of figures.

A 2 × 4 rectangle has 8 unit squares inside, so 2 × 4 = 8.

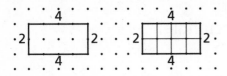

1. On your MathBoard, draw a 4 × 2 rectangle. How is the 4 × 2 rectangle similar to the 2 × 4 rectangle? How is it different?

_____

_____

_____

_____

2. How do the areas of the 2 × 4 and 4 × 2 rectangles compare?

_____

_____

Name _____   **Date** _____

Class Activity

▶ Factor the Tens to Multiply Ones and Tens

This 2 × 40 rectangle contains 8 groups of 10 square units,
so its area is 80 square units.

```
40 =      10        +        10        +        10        +        10
1 |   1 × 10 = 10  |   1 × 10 = 10  |   1 × 10 = 10  |   1 × 10 = 10   | 1
1 |   1 × 10 = 10  |   1 × 10 = 10  |   1 × 10 = 10  |   1 × 10 = 10   | 1
          10        +        10        +        10        +        10
```

3. How can we show this numerically? Complete the steps.

$2 \times 40 = (2 \times 1) \times (\underline{\hspace{1cm}} \times 10)$

$= (\underline{\hspace{1cm}} \times \underline{\hspace{1cm}}) \times (1 \times 10)$

$= \underline{\hspace{1cm}} \times 10 = 80$

4. On your MathBoard, draw a 40 × 2 rectangle and find
its area.

_____

5. How is the 40 × 2 rectangle similar to the 2 × 40 rectangle?
How is it different?

_____

_____

_____

_____

6. Write out the steps for finding 4 × 20 by factoring the tens.
Use your MathBoard if you need to.

_____

_____

_____

Multiplication Arrays

Class Activity

▶ **Model a Product of Tens**

7. Find the area of this 20 × 40 rectangle by dividing it into 10-by-10 squares of 100.

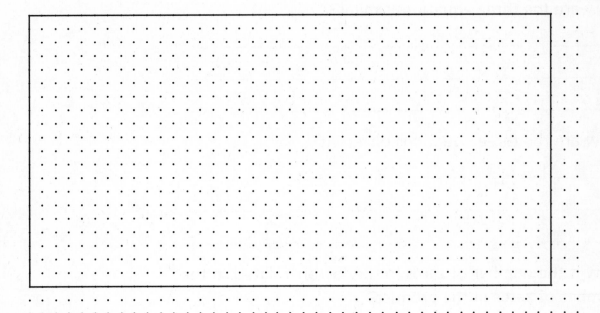

▶ **Factor the Tens**

8. Complete the steps to show your work in problem 7 numerically.

   20 × 40 = (_____ × 10) × (_____ × 10)

   = (_____ × _____) × (10 × 10)

   = _____ × 100

   = 800

9. Is it true that 20 × 40 = 40 × 20? Explain how you know.

   _____

10. Write out the steps for finding 40 × 20 by factoring the tens. Use your MathBoard if you need to.

   _____

   _____

▶ Compare Equations

In this lesson, you looked at these three equations.

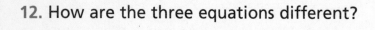

$$2 \times 4 = 8 \qquad 2 \times 40 = 80 \qquad 20 \times 40 = 800$$

11. How are the three equations similar?

_____

_____

_____

12. How are the three equations different?

_____

_____

_____

13. How is the number of zeros in the factors related to the number of zeros in the product?

_____

_____

_____

Name _____   Date _____

Vocabulary
factors
product

► Look for Patterns

Multiplying large numbers in your head is easier when you learn patterns of multiplication with tens.

Start with column A and look for the patterns used to get the expressions in each column. Complete the table.

Table 1

	A	B	C	D
	2 × 4	2 × 1 × 4 × 1	8 × 1	8
1.	2 × 40	2 × 1 × 4 × 10	8 × 10	_____
2.	20 × 40	2 × 10 × 4 × 10	_____	_____

3. How are the expressions in column B different from the expressions in column A?

_____

_____

_____

4. In column C, we see that each expression can be written as a number times a place value. Which of these **factors** gives more information about the size of the **product**?

_____

5. Why is 8 the first digit of the products in column D?

_____

6. Why are there different numbers of zeros in the products in column D?

_____

_____

Name _____

Date _____

Class Activity

▶ Compare Tables

Complete each table.

Table 2

	A	B	C	D
	4 × 3	4 × 1 × 3 × 1	12 × 1	12
7.	4 × 30	4 × 1 × 3 × 10	12 × 10	_____
8.	40 × 30	4 × 10 × 3 × 10	_____	_____

Table 3

	A	B	C	D
	5 × 8	5 × 1 × 8 × 1	40 × 1	40
9.	5 × 80	5 × 1 × 8 × 10	40 × 10	_____
10.	50 × 80	_____	_____	_____

11. Why do the products in Table 2 have more digits than the products in Table 1?

_____

_____

12. Why are there more zeros in the products in Table 3 than those in Table 2?

_____

_____

Mental Math and Multiplication with Tens

Class Activity

Vocabulary

area
square units

▶ **Explore the Area Model**

Copy this rectangle on your MathBoard.

```
         20              +    6
   ┌──────────────────┬─────────┐
 3 │· · · · · · · · · │· · · · · │
   │· · · · · · · · · │· · · · · │
   └──────────────────┴─────────┘
```

1. How many **square units** of **area** are there in the tens part of the drawing? _____

2. What multiplication equation gives the area of the tens part of the drawing? _____ Write this equation in its rectangle.

3. How many square units of area are there in the ones part? _____

4. What multiplication equation gives the area of the ones part? _____ Write this equation in its rectangle.

5. What is the total of the two areas? _____

6. How do you know that 78 is the correct product of 3×26?

_____

_____

7. Read problems A and B.

   A. Brad's photo album has 26 pages. Each page has 5 photos. How many photos are in Brad's album?

   B. Nick took 5 photos. Haley took 26 photos. How many more photos did Haley take than Nick?

   Which problem could you solve using the multiplication you just did? Explain why.

   _____

   _____

   _____

▶ Use Rectangles to Multiply

Draw a rectangle for each problem on your MathBoard.
Find the tens product, the ones product, and the total.

8. 8 × 38

_____

_____

_____

9. 3 × 29

_____

_____

_____

10. 4 × 28

_____

_____

_____

11. 5 × 46

_____

_____

_____

12. 2 × 38

_____

_____

_____

13. 3 × 28

_____

_____

_____

14. 5 × 30

_____

_____

_____

15. 5 × 28

_____

_____

_____

Solve each problem.

Show your work.

16. Claudia's father planted 8 rows of tomatoes in his garden. Each row had 12 plants. How many tomato plants were in Claudia's father's garden?

_____

17. The bakery can ice their cakes with chocolate, strawberry, or vanilla icing. The bakery has a total of 67 different ways to decorate iced cakes. How many different combinations of icing and decorations can the bakery make?

_____

18. Complete this word problem. Then solve it.

_____ has _____ boxes of _____.

There are _____ _____ in each box.

How many _____ does _____

have altogether? _____

Model One-Digit by Two-Digit Multiplication

▶ Numeric Multiplication Methods

You have used the area model to help you multiply.
In this lesson, you will learn some numeric multiplication
methods that are related to this area model.

Expanded Notation Method

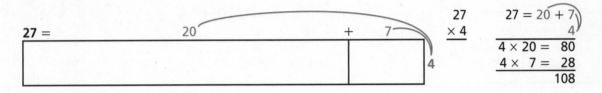

$$27 = 20 + 7$$

$$
\begin{array}{r}
27 \\
\times\, 4 \\
\end{array}
$$

$$
\begin{array}{r}
27 = 20 + 7 \\
4 \\
\hline
4 \times 20 = 80 \\
4 \times 7 = 28 \\
\hline
108 \\
\end{array}
$$

Algebraic Notation Method

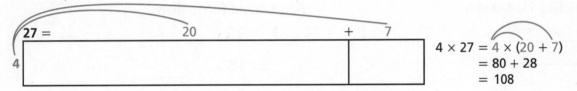

$$4 \times 27 = 4 \times (20 + 7)$$
$$= 80 + 28$$
$$= 108$$

▶ Connect the Multiplication Methods

Refer to the examples above.

1. What two values are added together to give the answer
   in the Expanded Notation Method?

   _____

2. What two values are added together to give the answer
   in the Algebraic Notation Method?

   _____

3. Choose one of the numeric methods and explain how it
   relates to the Rectangle Sections Method.

   _____

   _____

   _____

   _____

   _____

Class Activity

▶ Practice Different Methods

Fill in the blanks in the following solutions.

4. 3 × 76

Expanded Notation

$$76 = \underline{\qquad} + 6$$
$$\times\ 3 = \underline{\qquad}$$
$$\underline{\qquad}$$

$$3 \times \underline{\qquad} = \underline{\qquad}$$

$$\underline{\qquad} \times 6 = 18$$

$$\underline{\qquad}$$

Algebraic Notation

$$3 \cdot 76 = \underline{\qquad} \cdot (70 + 6)$$
$$= 210 + \underline{\qquad}$$
$$= \underline{\qquad}$$

5. 3 × 67

Expanded Notation

$$67 = \underline{\qquad} + 7$$
$$\times\ 3 = \underline{\qquad}$$

$$3 \times \underline{\qquad} = \underline{\qquad}$$

$$\underline{\qquad} \times 7 = 21$$

$$\underline{\qquad}$$

Algebraic Notation

$$3 \cdot 67 = 3 \cdot (\underline{\qquad} + \underline{\qquad})$$
$$= 180 + \underline{\qquad}$$
$$= \underline{\qquad}$$

Solve using a numeric method. Sketch a rectangle if necessary.

6. 8 × 53 = \underline{\qquad}

7. 6 × 72 = \underline{\qquad}

8. 6 × 27 = \underline{\qquad}

9. 5 × 64 = \underline{\qquad}

10. 5 × 46 = \underline{\qquad}

11. 7 × 92 = \underline{\qquad}

Class Activity

▶ Compare Multiplication Methods

Compare these methods for solving 7 × 23.

Method A	Method B	Method C	Method D	Method E
$23 = 20 + 3$	$23 = 20 + 3$	23	23	²23
$\times\ 7 =\qquad 7$	$\times\ 7 =\qquad 7$	$\times\quad 7$	$\times\quad 7$	$\times\quad 7$
$7 \times 20 = 140$	140	140	21	161
$7 \times\ \ 3 =\ \ 21$	21	21	140	
161	161	161	161	

1. How are all the methods similar? List at least two similarities.

_____

_____

_____

2. How are the methods different? List at least three differences.

_____

_____

_____

▶ Analyze the Shortcut Method

Method E can be broken down into 2 steps.

Method E:	Step 1	Step 2
	²23	²23
	$\times\quad 7$	$\times\quad 7$
	1	161

3. Where are the products 140 and 21 from methods A–D?

_____

_____

_____

▶Practice Multiplication

Solve using any method. Sketch a rectangle if necessary.
Check your answer by rounding and estimating.

4. $4 \times 68 =$ _____

5. $8 \times 72 =$ _____

6. $47 \times 9 =$ _____

7. $6 \times 54 =$ _____

8. $6 \times 23 =$ _____

9. $98 \times 2 =$ _____

10. $4 \times 82 =$ _____

11. $4 \times 86 =$ _____

Discuss Different Methods of Multiplication

▶ **Compare the Three Methods**

You can use the **Rectangle Sections Method** to multiply a one-digit number by a three-digit number.

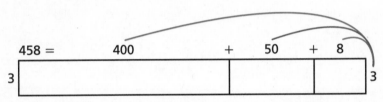

458 =	400	+	50	+	8	
3	3 × 400 = 1,200		3 × 50 = 150		3 × 8 = 24	3

$$\begin{array}{r} 1,200 \\ 150 \\ + \quad 24 \\ \hline 1,374 \end{array}$$

1. What are the two steps used to find the product of 3 × 458 using the Rectangle Sections Method?

_____

The **Expanded Notation Method** uses the same steps as the Rectangle Sections Method.

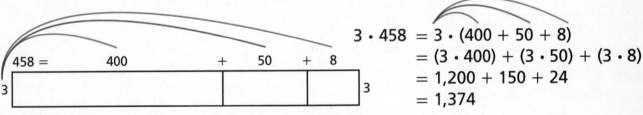

458 =	400	+	50	+	8	
3						3

$$458 = 400 + 50 + 8$$
$$\times \ 3 \qquad\qquad\qquad 3$$
$$\begin{array}{r} 3 \times 400 = 1,200 \\ 3 \times 50 = \quad 150 \\ 3 \times 8 = \quad\ 24 \\ \hline 1,374 \end{array}$$

2. What is the last step in the Expanded Notation Method and the Rectangle Sections Method?

_____

The **Algebraic Notation Method** uses expanded notation just like the other two methods. Even though the steps look different, they are the same as in the other methods.

458 =	400	+	50	+	8	
3						3

$$3 \cdot 458 = 3 \cdot (400 + 50 + 8)$$
$$= (3 \cdot 400) + (3 \cdot 50) + (3 \cdot 8)$$
$$= 1,200 + 150 + 24$$
$$= 1,374$$

3. What is the first step in all three methods?

_____

Use the rectangles to help you solve the multiplication problems.

1.

=		+	+

2.

=		+	+

3.

=		+	+

4.

=		+	+

Class Activity

▶Compare Multiplication Methods

Look at the drawing and the five numeric solutions
for 437 × 6.

437 =	400	+	30	+	7
6	6 × 400 = 2,400		6 × 30 = 180	6 × 7 = 42	

Method A	Method B	Method C	Method D	Method E
437 = 400 + 30 + 7	437 = 400 + 30 + 7	437	437	$\overset{2\ 4}{437}$
× 6 = 6	× 6 = 6	× 6	× 6	× 6
6 × 400 = 2,400	2,400	2,400	42	2,622
6 × 30 = 180	180	180	180	
6 × 7 = 42	42	42	2,400	
2,622	2,622	2,622	2,622	

1. How are the solutions similar? List at least two ways.

_____

_____

_____

2. How are the solutions different?
   List at least three comparisons between methods.

_____

_____

_____

_____

3. How do Methods A–D relate to the drawing? List at least two ways.

_____

_____

_____

► **Analyze the Shortcut Method**

Look at this breakdown of solution steps for Method E.

Step 1	Step 2	Step 3

$$\begin{array}{r} \overset{1}{363} \\ \times\ \ 5 \\ \hline 5 \end{array}$$

$$\begin{array}{r} \overset{3\,1}{363} \\ \times\ \ 5 \\ \hline 15 \end{array}$$

$$\begin{array}{r} \overset{3\,1}{363} \\ \times\ \ 5 \\ \hline 1{,}815 \end{array}$$

4. Describe what happens in Step 1.

_____

_____

_____

5. Describe what happens in Step 2.

_____

_____

_____

6. Describe what happens in Step 3.

_____

_____

_____

Practice the Shortcut Method on these problems.

7. $\begin{array}{r} 415 \\ \times\ \ 3 \\ \hline 1{,}245 \end{array}$
   8. $\begin{array}{r} 768 \\ \times\ \ 9 \\ \hline 6{,}912 \end{array}$
   9. $\begin{array}{r} 632 \\ \times\ \ 7 \\ \hline 4{,}424 \end{array}$
   10. $\begin{array}{r} 349 \\ \times\ \ 6 \\ \hline 2{,}094 \end{array}$

► Divide Hundreds

In mathematics, special words are used to describe parts of a problem.

Discuss these multiplication and division words.

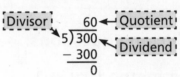

Multiplication Words

$$\begin{array}{r} 60 \\ \times\ 5 \\ \hline 300 \end{array}$$ ← Factor
← Factor
← Product

Factor → $\begin{array}{r} 60 \\ 5)\overline{300} \\ -\ 300 \\ \hline 0 \end{array}$ ← Product

Division Words

Divisor → $\begin{array}{r} 60 \\ 5)\overline{300} \\ -\ 300 \\ \hline 0 \end{array}$ ← Quotient
← Dividend

1. Describe the relationships among these 5 words in rectangles.

_____

_____

► Three Division Methods

The sidewalk crew knows that the sidewalk is 330 square feet. The sidewalk is 5 feet wide. How long is the sidewalk? Brianna, Carlos, and Michelle each use a different method to find the answer.

Brianna's Rectangle Sections Method

a.

$$5\ \boxed{\ 330\ }$$

b.

60
$$5\ \boxed{\begin{array}{r} 330 \\ -\ 300 \\ \hline 30 \end{array}}$$

c.

60 +
$$5\ \boxed{\begin{array}{r|r} 330 & \\ -\ 300 & \\ \hline 30 & \end{array}}$$

d.

60 +
$$5\ \boxed{\begin{array}{r|r} 330 & 30 \\ -\ 300 & \\ \hline 30 & \end{array}}$$

e.

60 +   6
$$5\ \boxed{\begin{array}{r|r} 330 & 30 \\ -\ 300 & -\ 30 \\ \hline 30 & \end{array}}$$

f.

60 +   6 = 66
$$5\ \boxed{\begin{array}{r|r} 330 & 30 \\ -\ 300 & -\ 30 \\ \hline 30 & 0 \end{array}}$$

Carlos's Expanded Notation Method

g.

$$5)\overline{330}$$

h.

60
$$5)\overline{\begin{array}{r} 330 \\ -\ 300 \end{array}}$$

i.

60
$$5)\overline{\begin{array}{r} 330 \\ -\ 300 \\ \hline 30 \end{array}}$$

j.

6
60
$$5)\overline{\begin{array}{r} 330 \\ -\ 300 \\ \hline 30 \end{array}}$$

k.

6
60
$$5)\overline{\begin{array}{r} 330 \\ -\ 300 \\ \hline 30 \\ -\ 30 \\ \hline 0 \end{array}}$$

l.

6 ⎤ 66
60 ⎦
$$5)\overline{\begin{array}{r} 330 \\ -\ 300 \\ \hline 30 \\ -\ 30 \\ \hline 0 \end{array}}$$

Class Activity

▶ Three Division Methods (Continued)

Michelle's Digit-by-Digit Method

m.

$$5\overline{)330}$$

n.

$$\begin{array}{r} 6 \\ 5\overline{)330} \\ -30 \\ \hline \end{array}$$

o.

$$\begin{array}{r} 6 \\ 5\overline{)330} \\ -30 \\ \hline 3 \end{array}$$

p.

$$\begin{array}{r} 6 \\ 5\overline{)330} \\ -30 \\ \hline 30 \end{array}$$

q.

$$\begin{array}{r} 66 \\ 5\overline{)330} \\ -30 \\ \hline 30 \end{array}$$

r.

$$\begin{array}{r} 66 \\ 5\overline{)330} \\ -30 \\ \hline 30 \\ -30 \\ \hline 0 \end{array}$$

Answer the following questions.

2. How are their methods alike?

_____

_____

3. How are their methods different?

_____

_____

4. What other methods do you know that could solve this problem?

_____

_____

5. How do the division methods relate to the multiplication methods below?

Rectangle Sections Method

$$\begin{array}{c|c|c} & 60 & + & 6 \\ \hline 5 & 60 \times 5 & 5 \times 6 \\ & = 300 & = 30 \end{array}$$

$$\begin{array}{r} 300 \\ + 30 \\ \hline 330 \end{array}$$

Expanded Notation Method

$$\begin{array}{r} 66 = 60 + 6 \\ 5 = 5 \\ \hline 5 \times 60 = 300 \\ 5 \times 6 = 30 \\ \hline 330 \end{array}$$

_____

_____

Class Activity

Name _____ Date _____

▶ Estimate Products

It is easier to **estimate** the product of a two-digit number and a one-digit number when you think about the two multiples of ten close to the two-digit number. This is shown in the drawings below.

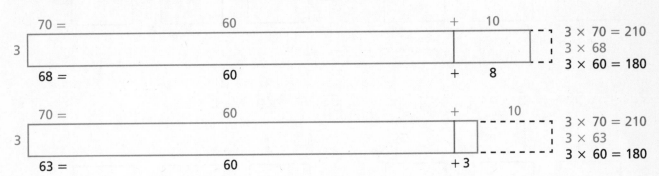

1. In each drawing, find the rectangles that represent 3×70 and 3×60. These rectangles "frame" the rectangles for 3×63 and 3×68. Find the values of 3×70 and 3×60.

   $3 \times 70 =$ _____ $3 \times 60 =$ _____

2. Look at the rectangle that represents 3×68. Is 3×68 closer to 3×60 or to 3×70? So is 3×68 closer to 180 or 210?

   _____

3. Look at the rectangle that represents 3×63. Is 3×63 closer to 3×60 or to 3×70? Is 3×63 closer to 180 or 210?

   _____

4. Explain how to use **rounding** to estimate the product of a one-digit number and a two-digit number.

   _____

   _____

   _____

Use compatible numbers to estimate each quotient.

5.   177 ÷ 3

[ ] ÷ [ ] = [ ]

6.   915 ÷ 8

[ ] ÷ [ ] = [ ]

7.   196 ÷ 5

[ ] ÷ [ ] = [ ]

8.   124 ÷ 6

[ ] ÷ [ ] = [ ]

9.   564 ÷ 7

[ ] ÷ [ ] = [ ]

10.   384 ÷ 4

[ ] ÷ [ ] = [ ]

Solve.

11. A teacher needs to order 5 book sets for her class. The total cost of the book sets were $276. About how much was each book set? Explain your thinking.

_____

_____

_____

Estimate Products and Quotients

Class Activity

Name _____

Date _____

▶The Puzzled Penguin

Dear Students,
Today I had to solve this problem.

Barron counts 37 tiles across the floor and 6 tiles down one side. How many floor tiles are there in the room?

37
+ 6
_____
43 floor tiles

Is my answer correct? If not, please help me understand why it is wrong.

Thank you,
The Puzzled Penguin

1. Is the Puzzled Penguin correct? Explain your thinking.

_____

_____

_____

_____

_____

2. Use a drawing to show could you use a rectangular array to help you solve the problem.

3. Which two operations can you use to solve this problem?

_____

4. How can you use estimation to check if your answer is reasonable?

_____

_____

_____

Class Activity

▶ The Puzzled Penguin

Dear Students,

Today I had to solve this problem.

> Ariana works at her family's fruit stand. She was asked to bag 32 grapefruits. Each large bag can hold 4 grapefruits. How many large bags will Ariana need to fit all the grapefruits?

$32 - 4 = 28$ $28 - 4 = 24$ $24 - 4 = 20$ $20 - 4 = 16$

$16 - 4 = 12$ $12 - 4 = 8$ $8 - 4 = 4$ 7 bags

Is my answer correct? If not, please help me understand why it is wrong.

Thank you,

The Puzzled Penguin

5. Is the Puzzled Penguin correct? Explain your thinking.

_____

_____

_____

_____

6. Use a drawing to show how could you use counters to help you solve the problem.

7. Which two operations can you use to solve this problem?

_____

8. How can you use multiplication to check if your answer is correct?

_____

Class Activity

► **Explore Change Over Time**

Look at the function table and answer the questions.

Money in Savings Account

Week	Amount of Money
1	$210
2	$225
3	$240
4	$255
5	$270

1. What information does this function table show you?

_____

_____

2. How does the money amount change in the savings account from week to week?

_____

3. Predict how much money there would be in the savings account after week 10.

_____

4. Explain how you found the answer to exercise 3.

_____

_____

_____

_____

5. Do you think the same pattern and function rule will continue over time? Explain.

_____

Class Activity

Sam kept track of an animal's weight at the zoo.
Here is the data he collected to the nearest pound.

Month	Weight (kilograms)
January	48
February	56
March	64
April	72
May	80

►Practice with Change Over Time

6. **Make a line graph with the data above.** on centimeter grid paper.

7. What do you notice about the data over time?

_____

8. What was the change in weight between February and March?

_____

9. Predict what the weight of the animal will be in June?

_____

10. Explain your thinking for exercise 9.

_____

_____

Line Graphs

Glossary

A

acute angle An angle whose measure is less than 90°.

acute triangle A triangle in which the measure of each angle is less than 90°.

addend A number to be added.

Example: $8 + 4 = 12$

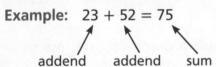
addend   addend

addition A mathematical operation that combines two or more numbers.

Example: $23 + 52 = 75$

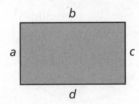
addend   addend   sum

adjacent (sides) Two sides that meet at a point.

Example: Sides *a* and *b* are adjacent.

A.M. The time period between midnight and noon.

angle A figure formed by two rays or two line segments that meet at an endpoint.

area The number of square units in a region

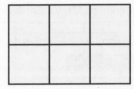

The area of the rectangle is 6 square units.

array An arrangement of objects, pictures, or numbers in columns and rows.

Associative Property of Addition (Grouping Property of Addition) The property which states that changing the way in which addends are grouped does not change the sum.

Example: $(2 + 3) + 1 = 2 + (3 + 1)$

$$5 + 1 = 2 + 4$$

$$6 = 6$$

Associative Property of Multiplication (Grouping Property of Multiplication) The property which states that changing the way in which factors are grouped does not change the product.

Example: $(2 \times 3) \times 4 = 2 \times (3 \times 4)$

$$6 \times 4 = 2 \times 12$$

$$24 = 24$$

Glossary (Continued)

axis (plural: **axes**) A reference line for a graph. A bar graph has 2 axes; one is horizontal and the other is vertical.

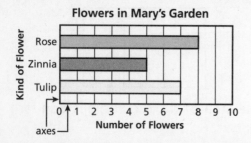

Flowers in Mary's Garden

B

bar graph A graph that uses bars to show data. The bars may be horizontal or vertical.

Canned Goods at Turner's Market

base (of a geometric figure) The bottom side of a 2-D figure or the bottom face of a 3-D figure.

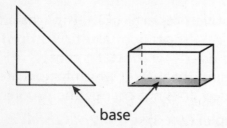

base

C

calculator A tool used to perform mathematical operations.

capacity The amount a container can hold.

cell A rectangle in a table where a column and row meet.

Coin Toss

	Heads	Tails
Sam	11	6	} cell
Zoe	9	10

centimeter (cm) A metric unit used to measure length.

100 cm = 1 m

circle A plane figure that forms a closed path so that all points on the path are the same distance from a point called the center.

circle graph A graph that represents data as parts of a whole.

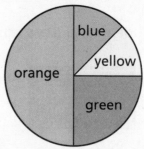

Jacket Colors in Ms. Timmer's Class

circumference The distance around a circle, about $3\frac{1}{7}$ times the diameter.

column A vertical group of cells in a table.

Coin Toss

	Heads	Tails
Sam	11	6
Zoe	9	10

column

Commutative Property of Addition (Order Property of Addition) The property which states that changing the order of addends does not change the sum.

Example: $3 + 7 = 7 + 3$

$10 = 10$

Commutative Property of Multiplication (Order Property of Multiplication) The property which states that changing the order of factors does not change the product.

Example: $5 \times 4 = 4 \times 5$

$20 = 20$

comparison bars Bars that represent the larger amount, smaller amount, and difference in a comparison problem.

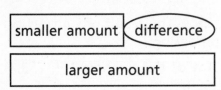

In Volume 2, we use comparison bars for multiplication.

cone A solid figure that has a circular base and comes to a point called the vertex.

congruent figures Figures that have the same size and shape.

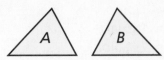

Triangles A and B are congruent.

coordinates The numbers in an ordered pair that locate a point on a coordinate grid. The first number is the distance across and the second number is the distance up.

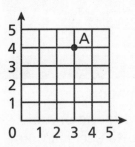

The coordinates 3 and 4 in the ordered pair (3, 4) locate Point A on the coordinate grid.

coordinate grid A grid formed by two perpendicular number lines in which every point is assigned an ordered pair of numbers.

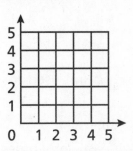

cube A solid figure that has six square faces of equal size.

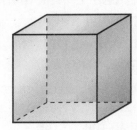

Glossary (Continued)

cup (c) A customary unit of measurement used to measure capacity.

2 cups = 1 pint
4 cups = 1 quart
16 cups = 1 gallon

cylinder A solid figure with two congruent circular or elliptical faces and one curved surface.

D

data Pieces of information.

decimal A number with one or more digits to the right of a decimal point.

Examples: 1.23 and 0.3

decimal point The dot that separates the whole number from the decimal part.

1.23

decimal point

decimeter (dm) A metric unit used to measure length

1 decimeter = 10 centimeters

degree (°) A unit for measuring angles or temperature.

degrees Celsius (°C) The metric unit for measuring temperature.

degrees Fahrenheit (°F) The customary unit of temperature.

denominator The bottom number in a fraction that shows the total number of equal parts in the whole.

Example: $\frac{1}{3}$ ←—— denominator

diagonal A line segment that connects two corners of a figure and is not a side of the figure.

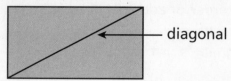

diameter A line segment that connects two points on a circle and also passes through the center of the circle. The term is also used to describe the length of such a line segment.

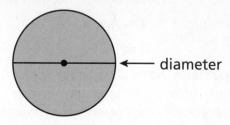

difference The result of subtraction or of comparing.

digit Any of the symbols 0, 1, 2, 3, 4, 5, 6, 7, 8, 9.

dividend The number that is divided in division.

Examples:

$12 \div 3 = 4$ $\qquad$ $3\overline{)12}^{\,4}$

dividend $\qquad\qquad$ dividend

division The mathematical operation that separates an amount into smaller equal groups to find the number of groups or the number in each group.

Example: $12 \div 3 = 4$ is a division number sentence.

divisor The number that you divide by in division.

Example: $12 \div 3 = 4$ $\quad$ $3\overline{)12}^{\,4}$

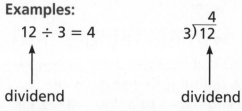

divisor $\quad$ divisor

E

edge The line segment where two faces of a solid figure meet.

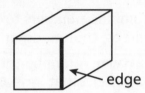
edge

elapsed time The time that passes between the beginning and the end of an activity.

endpoint The point at either end of a line segment or the beginning point of a ray.

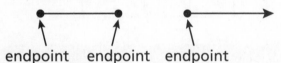
endpoint   endpoint   endpoint

equation A mathematical sentence with an equals sign.

Examples: $11 + 22 = 33$
$75 - 25 = 50$

equilateral triangle A triangle whose sides are all the same length.

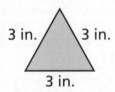
3 in.   3 in.
3 in.

equivalent Equal, or naming the same amount.

equivalent fractions Fractions that name the same amount.

Example: $\frac{1}{2}$ and $\frac{2}{4}$

equivalent fractions

estimate About how many or about how much.

even number A whole number that is a multiple of 2. The ones digit in an even number is 0, 2, 4, 6, or 8.

event In probability, a possible outcome.

expanded form A number written to show the value of each of its digits.

Examples:
$347 = 300 + 40 + 7$
$347 = 3$ hundreds $+ 4$ tens $+ 7$ ones

expression A combination of numbers, variables, and/or operation signs. An expression does not have an equals sign.

Examples: $4 + 7$ $a - 3$

F

face A flat surface of a solid figure.

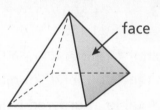
face

factors Numbers that are multiplied to give a product.

Example: $4 \times 5 = 20$

factor   factor   product

flip To reflect a figure over a line. The size and shape of the figure remain the same.

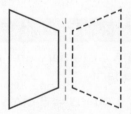

foot (ft) A customary unit used to measure length.

1 foot = 12 inches

Glossary (Continued)

formula An equation with variables that describes a rule.

The formula for the area of a rectangle is:

$A = l \times w$

where A is the area, l is the length, and w is the width.

fraction A number that names part of a whole or part of a set.

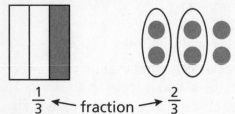

$$\frac{1}{3} \leftarrow \text{fraction} \rightarrow \frac{2}{3}$$

front-end estimation A method of estimating that keeps the largest place value in a number and drops the rest.

Example:
$$\begin{array}{rcl} 527 & \rightarrow & 500 \\ + 673 & \rightarrow & + 600 \\ \hline & & 1,100 \end{array}$$

The 5 in 527 is the "front end" number
The 6 in 673 is the "front end" number

function table A table of ordered pairs that shows a function.

For every input number, there is only one possible output number.

Rule: add 2	
Input	Output
1	3
2	4
3	5
4	6

G

gallon (gal) A customary unit used to measure capacity.

1 gallon = 4 quarts = 8 pints = 16 cups

gram (g) A metric unit of mass, about 1 paper clip.

1,000 grams = 1 kilogram

greater than (>) A symbol used to compare two numbers.

Example: 6 > 5

6 is greater than 5.

group To combine numbers to form new tens, hundreds, thousands, and so on.

growing pattern A number or geometric pattern that increases.

Examples: 2, 4, 6, 8, 10…
1, 2, 5, 10, 17…

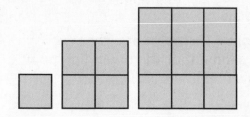

H

height A measurement of vertical length, or how tall something is.

horizontal Extending in two directions, left and right.

horizontal bar graph A bar graph with horizontal bars.

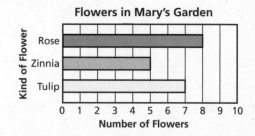

hundredth One of the equal parts when a whole is divided into 100 equal parts.

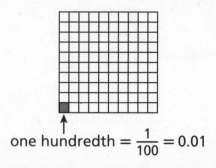

$$\text{one hundredth} = \frac{1}{100} = 0.01$$

I

improper fraction A fraction in which the numerator is equal to or is greater than the denominator. Improper fractions are equal to or greater than 1. $\frac{5}{5}$ and $\frac{8}{3}$ are improper fractions.

inch (in.) A customary unit used to measure length.

12 inches = 1 foot

isosceles triangle A triangle that has at least two sides of the same length.

K

key A part of a map, graph, or chart that explains what symbols mean.

kilogram (kg) A metric unit of mass.

1 kilogram = 1,000 grams

kilometer (km) A metric unit of length.

1 kilometer = 1,000 meters

L

less than (<) A symbol used to compare numbers.

Example: 5 < 6

5 *is less than* 6.

line A straight path that goes on forever in opposite directions.

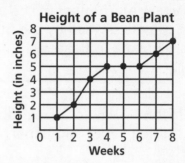

line graph A graph that uses a straight line or a broken line to show changes in data.

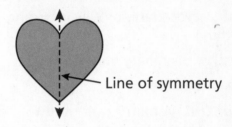

Height of a Bean Plant

line of symmetry A line on which a figure can be folded so that the two halves match exactly.

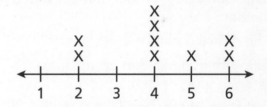

Line of symmetry

line plot A way to show data using a number line.

line segment A part of a line. A line segment has two endpoints.

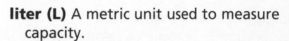

liter (L) A metric unit used to measure capacity.

1 liter = 1,000 milliliters

Glossary (Continued)

M

mass The amount of matter in an object.

mean (average) The sum of the values in a set of data divided by the number of pieces of data in the set.

Example: $3 + 5 + 4 + 8 = 20$
$20 \div 4 = 5$ 5 is the mean

mental math A way to solve problems without using pencil and paper, or a calculator.

meter (m) A metric unit used to measure length.

1 meter = 100 centimeters

method A procedure, or way, of doing something.

mile (mi) A customary unit of length.

1 mile = 5,280 feet

milliliter (mL) A metric unit used to measure capacity.

1,000 milliliters = 1 liter

mixed number A whole number and a fraction.

$1\frac{3}{4}$ is a mixed number.

mode The number that occurs most often in a set of data.

In this set of numbers {3, 4, 5, 5, 5, 7, 8}, 5 is the mode.

multiple A number that is the product of the given number and another number.

multiplication A mathematical operation that combines equal groups.

Example: $4 \times 3 = 12$

factor   factor   product

$3 + 3 + 3 + 3 = 12$

4 times

N

net A flat pattern that can be folded to make a solid figure.

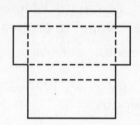

This net can be folded into a rectangular prism.

number line A line on which numbers are assigned to lengths.

numerator The top number in a fraction that shows the number of equal parts counted.

Example: $\frac{1}{3}$ ← numerator

O

obtuse angle An angle that measures more than 90° but less than 180°.

obtuse triangle A triangle with one angle that measures more than 90°.

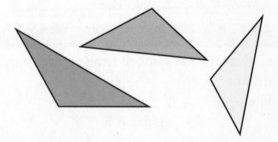

odd number A whole number that is not a multiple of 2. The ones digit in an odd number is 1, 3, 5, 7, or 9.

opposite sides Sides that are across from each other; they do not meet at a point.

Example: Sides *a* and *c* are opposite.

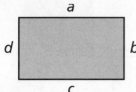

ordered pair A pair of numbers such as (3, 4) in which one number is considered to be first and the other number second. They can name a point on a coordinate grid.

ordinal numbers Numbers used to show order or position.

Example: first, second, fifth

ounce (oz) A customary unit used to measure weight.

16 ounces = 1 pound

P

parallel lines Two lines that are everywhere the same distance apart.

parallelogram A quadrilateral with both pairs of opposite sides parallel.

partner One of two numbers that add to make a total.

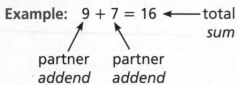

perimeter The distance around the outside of a figure.

perpendicular Two lines or line segments that cross or meet to form right angles.

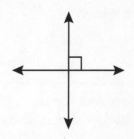

pictograph A graph that uses pictures or symbols to represent data.

pint (pt) A customary unit used to measure capacity.

1 pint = 2 cups

place value The value assigned to the place that a digit occupies in a number.

9   6   2
↑   ↑   ↑
hundreds tens   ones

place value drawing A drawing that represents a number. Hundreds are represented by boxes, tens by vertical lines, and ones by small circles.

plane figure A closed figure that has two dimensions.

Glossary (Continued)

P.M. The time period between noon and midnight.

pound (lb) A customary unit used to measure weight.

1 pound = 16 ounces

prism A solid figure with two parallel congruent bases, and rectangles or parallelograms for faces. A prism is named by the shape of its bases.

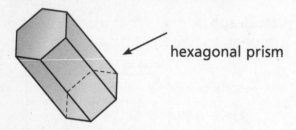

hexagonal prism

probability The chance of an event occurring.

product The answer when you multiply numbers.

Example: 4 × 7 = 28

factor   factor   product

proof drawing A drawing used to show that an answer is correct.

249
+ 386
 11
635

pyramid A solid figure with one base and whose other faces are triangles with a common vertex. A pyramid is named by the shape of its base.

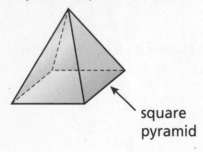

square pyramid

Q

quadrilateral A figure with four sides.

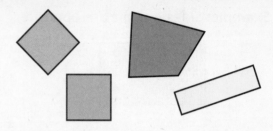

quart (qt) A customary unit used to measure capacity.

1 quart = 4 cups

quotient The answer when you divide numbers.

Examples:

$$35 \div 7 = 5 \qquad 7\overline{)35}\;\overset{5}{}\; \leftarrow \text{quotient}$$

quotient

R

radius A line segment that connects the center of a circle to any point on the circle. The term is also used to describe the length of such a line segment.

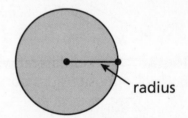

radius

range The difference between the greatest number and the least number in a set of data.

In this set of numbers {12, 15, 18, 19, 20}, the range is 20 − 12 or 8

ray A part of a line that has one endpoint and goes on forever in one direction.

rectangle A parallelogram that has 4 right angles.

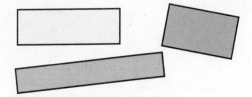

rectangular prism A prism with six rectangular faces.

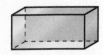

rectangular pyramid A pyramid with a rectangular base and four triangular faces.

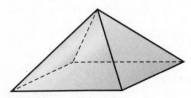

repeating pattern A pattern consisting of a group of numbers, letters, or figures that repeat.

Examples: 1, 2, 1, 2, …
           A, B, C, A, B, C, …

rhombus A parallelogram with congruent sides.

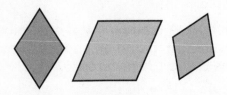

right angle An angle that measures 90°.

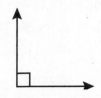

right triangle A triangle with one right angle.

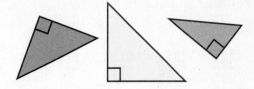

round To find about how many or how much by expressing a number to the nearest ten, hundred, thousand, and so on.

route The path taken to get to a location.

row A horizontal group of cells in a table.

Coin Toss

	Heads	Tails
Sam	11	6
Zoe	9	10

} row

S

scale An arrangement of numbers in order with equal intervals.

scalene triangle A triangle with sides of three different lengths.

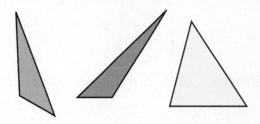

Glossary (Continued)

shrinking pattern A number or geometric pattern that decreases.

Examples: 15, 12, 9, 6, 3,…

25, 20, 16, 13, 11,…

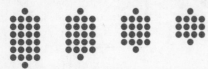

side (of a figure) A line segment that makes up a figure.

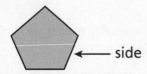

simplify To write an equivalent fraction with a smaller numerator and denominator.

slide To move a figure along a line in any direction. The size and shape of the figure remain the same.

solid figure A figure that has three dimensions.

sphere A solid figure shaped like a ball.

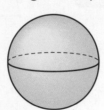

square A rectangle with four sides of the same length.

square number A product of a whole number and itself.

Example: $4 \times 4 = 16$

square number

square pyramid A pyramid with a square base and four triangular faces.

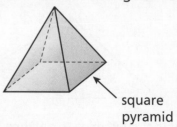

square pyramid

standard form The name of a number written using digits.

Example: 1,829

straight angle An angle that measures 180°.

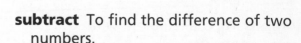

subtract To find the difference of two numbers.

Example: $18 - 11 = 7$

subtraction A mathematical operation on a sum (total) and an addend, which can be called the difference.

Example: $43 - 40 = 3$

sum The answer when adding two or more addends.

Example: $37 + 52 = 89$

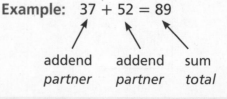

addend   addend   sum
partner   *partner*   *total*

survey A method of collecting information.

symmetry A figure has symmetry if it can be folded along a line so that the two halves match exactly.

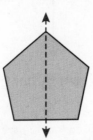

T

table An easy to read arrangement of data, usually in rows and columns.

Coin Toss

	Heads	Tails
Sam	11	6
Zoe	9	10

tally marks Short line segments drawn in groups of 5. Each mark including the slanted marks stands for 1 unit.

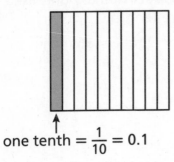 means 13

tenth One of the equal parts when a whole is divided into ten equal parts.

one tenth = $\frac{1}{10}$ = 0.1

thermometer A tool for measuring temperature.

total The answer when adding two or more addends. The sum of two or more numbers.

Example: 672 + 228 = 900

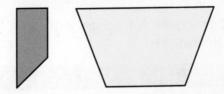

partner partner   total
addend   addend   sum

trapezoid A quadrilateral with exactly one pair of parallel sides.

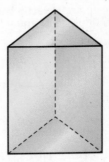

triangular prism A solid figure with two triangular faces and three rectangular faces.

Example:

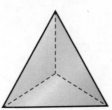

triangular pyramid A pyramid whose base is a triangle.

turn To rotate a figure around a point. The size and shape of the figure remains the same.

U

...ngroup To open up 1 in a given place to make 10 of the next smaller place value in order to subtract.

unit fraction A fraction with a numerator of 1.

V

Venn diagram A diagram that uses circles to show the relationship among sets of objects.

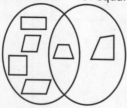

At least one pair of parallel sides   Exactly two sides of equal length

vertex A point where sides, rays, or edges meet.

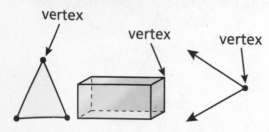

vertex   vertex   vertex

vertical Extending in two directions, up and down.

vertical bar graph A bar graph with vertical bars.

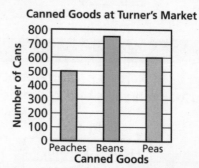

Canned Goods at Turner's Market

W

weight The measure of how heavy something is.

word form A name of a number written using words instead of digits.

Example: Nine hundred eighty-four

Y

yard (yd) A customary unit used to measure length.

1 yard = 3 feet = 36 inches